MY WILD YOUTH IN GL

by
"Daredevil"
Dick Sheppard

First Published in Great Britain in 2010 by
Tweenbrook Publishing
389 Stroud Road
Gloucester
GL4 0DA

ISBN 978-0-9565329-0-9

Produced by
Windmill Print & Graphics
Stroud, Gloucestershire
GL5 5BH

DEDICATION

To my parents, Bill and 'T', who gave me the most precious of all gifts – a chance at life, but who probably should have smacked me more than they did!

On the other hand, if they had subdued me, then this book would not have been written!

My mothers' nearest sibling was Jack, who called her "Itsy Tisty Spider" which became abbreviated to Tissie. She did not like this at all and insisted that it be further reduced to 'T', which remained her name for over 80 years!

Apparently on the occasion of their wedding, the Vicar asked my father if he would take Florence Eva Rice to be his lawful wedded wife, he said "Who?", because he had only ever known her as 'T'!

My father and mother enjoying their sport.
They ran the tennis club at the Oval off Tuffley Avenue.

FOREWORD

In our peer group, Dick was definitely different. It was wartime and there were no extra school sporting activities, such as mountaineering or abseiling. These sorts of things just did not happen, but they happened for him. He was always at the forefront of any activity and quite often pushed the limits to the extreme, but always seemed to survive!

Serbert Lane

Fellow Student 1941 - 1947

By the same author
(and in conjunction with the co-author Jacquie De Creed)

CLOSE to the EDGE

a duo-biography of
two record holding stunt artists

TABLE OF CONTENTS

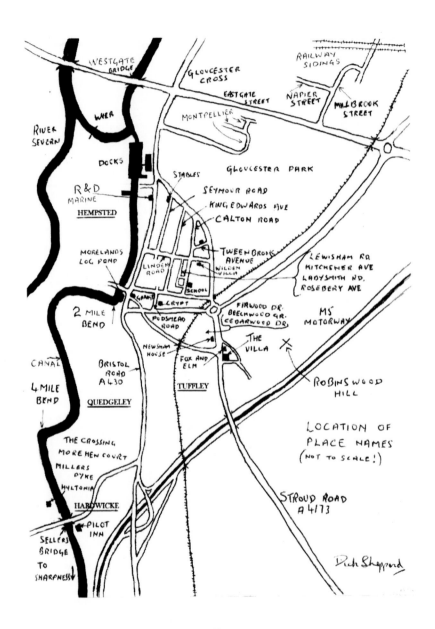

WESTGATE BRIDGE

GLOUCESTER CROSS

RAILWAY SIDINGS

EASTGATE STREET

NAPIER STREET

MILLBROOK STREET

MONTPELLIER

WEIR

RIVER SEVERN

DOCKS

GLOUCESTER PARK

STABLES

SEYMOUR ROAD

R & D MARINE

KING EDWARDS AVE

HEMPSTED

CALTON ROAD

TWEENBROOK AVENUE

MORELANDS LOG POND

LINDEN ROAD

WILDEN VILLA

LEWISHAM RD.
KITCHENER AVE
LADYSMITH RD.
ROSEBERY AVE

SCHOOL

GARAGE

CRYPT

2 MILE BEND

PODSMEAD ROAD

FIRWOOD DR.
BEECHWOOD GR.
CEDARWOOD DR.

M5 MOTORWAY

CANAL

NEWSHAM HOUSE

THE VILLA

4 MILE BEND

BRISTOL ROAD A430

FOX AND ELM

ROBINSWOOD HILL

QUEDGELEY

TUFFLEY

THE CROSSING
MOREHEN COURT
MILLERS PYKE
HYLTONIA

LOCATION OF PLACE NAMES
(NOT TO SCALE!)

HARDWICKE

PILOT INN

STROUD ROAD A4173

SELLERS BRIDGE TO SHARPNESS

Dick Sheppard

8

INTRODUCTION

At 7:15 a.m., on the morning of May 20th 1930, a 7 lbs baby was born to Bill and 'T' Sheppard at No. 18 Tweenbrook Avenue, Gloucester.

A few hours later, on that very same day, another world-changing occurrence took place. It was the world's first public television broadcast by the BBC from Alexandra Palace, London.

Not many people will have seen it, as there were so few receivers. The 1939-1945 hostilities further delayed its development and it was not until the Queen's coronation in 1947 that there was a good viewing audience. In fact every member of the British public seemed to know of someone who owned a black and white 9 inch TV set. Consequently the whole population were gathered in any neighbour's parlour who happened to have one, for that momentous occasion.

As TV and I were born on the same day, it was quite relevant that we would grow up together. Consequently, I did interviews and shows for the British Broadcasting Corporation and on the introduction of Independent Television, I worked for all of the following, Tyne Tees, Harlech, Border, Anglia, Midlands, Central, London Weekend, Thames and Southern Television. Some of these companies have since ceased while others have combined into four main groups.

There have also been many worldwide TV Stations in 35 different countries, but my main employer has always been 'Auntie' BBC, where I was resident stuntman/stunt arranger for many programmes such as Seaside Special, That's Life, It Could be You, Not the Nine O'clock News, Kelly Montieth Show and the Late Late Breakfast Show.

So if you are wondering what the formative years of such a character were like, and to learn how they affected someone who was born, educated and initially worked in Gloucestershire, then this is the book for you.

On reflection, my career evolved as it did due to the activities of my youth. They were frustrating and fast moving times, but on recalling them I realized what freedom I enjoyed, and could not help be aware of the difference in parent's attitude over just one generation, culminating in today's 'cotton wool' society. I wonder if this is one of the causes of the increase in gun and knife crime among our youth today.

The action portrayed in films these days is mostly computer generated. I think that producers would have difficulty in finding outgoing characters able to produce hair-raising live performances.

To learn details of my wild youth from previously untold stories, then read on. It may also help indicate how your offspring's career may develop if they show similar traits to mine!

My first toy

Walking up the "motorway" which was the long boring path at Tweenbrook Ave.

CHAPTER 1

PRE-SCHOOL DAYS - 1930

One of my very earliest recollections was my first toy, which I remember was a wooden horse, which was prophetic indeed as horses featured so prominently in my future. I also vividly remember what happened to it! My parents took it off me and gave it to Ivor, the son of Mr. and Mrs. Prosser, who were the bridge keepers of Sellars Bridge, Hardwicke. He was a little older than me and had made a stable in the front garden of the bridge keepers' house, and my parents donated my horse to the project!

My next toy, which also turned out to be very relevant, was a pedal car. The garden path was quite straight from the house to the end of the plot and it was boring, just like a motorway. I looked forward to wet days, when I was allowed to drive round and round the kitchen and scullery and in and out of the kitchen table legs. I could not go into the dining room because there was a nine inch step in between. This was typical of the houses at the time and I have wondered since why, just for the sake of saving a few hundred bricks, they could not have been built level. This step at least saved the dining table from the scratches that the kitchen table got! (I had not yet learned how to build ramps).

The parlour had a gas fire, the dining room had an anthracite stove and the kitchen had a coal fired range, on which a lot of the cooking was done. The bathroom upstairs had a frightening looking gas fired geyser. I describe the heating arrangements of each room because my parents tried to sell me the idea that Santa Claus came down the chimney. This I did not believe for one moment! I immediately looked up all of the flues and each one entered the chimney via a four inch pipe; I already knew that Santa was quite portly! They conceded that they had been teasing and that he actually came through the front door, which, I suppose, he did.

My father was quite a King Solomon. He settled most family disputes with complete fairness. An example of this was when my sister and I had received Easter eggs each from our aunt in Adderbury. Unfortunately one had become broken in the post and we were arguing as to whose egg it was. My father heard the noise, to settle the argument he simply crushed it and said, "Now choose!"

He asked us children one day, while we were staying at the summer bungalow, if we wanted to go for a walk. We both said yes, so he told us to get washed and dressed. As usual we were both in our swimwear. I was busy doing something so that when my father and sister were ready to go, I was not! He looked at me and asked if I had washed yet, I said I hadn't, so he threw a bucket full of water over me and they went for their walk without me! I was shocked at the time, but on reflection, it taught a good lesson on punctuality!

The model that my father made from the builders' scale model.

My next childhood toy was a three foot long, 3-masted schooner, which he made and I still have it.

The glass plaque that was attached to the ship builders scale model.

The recently renovated Lucy Pillar Warehouse visible from Llanthony Road

The schooner Lucy Johns photographed during her short life.

There was a local family called Lucy. Their trade was warehousing and shipping and they gave their name to the Lucy and Pillar warehouse, which is still there in Merchants Road, the pillars of which can be seen looking south from Llanthony Bridge.

In 1906 they commissioned a boatyard at Appledore in Devon to build them a new boat. To get the shape of the hull right, the builders first made one half of a scale model. This gave them all the measurements they needed. After construction it was usual for the boatyard to donate this model to the owners, partly as a souvenir and partly to show that the design would not be copied.

The schooner was named the Lucy Johns, but in 1910 she was lost with all hands in a storm in the Irish Sea. The owners threw out the model, so my father salvaged it, and hung it on his office wall. It was mounted on a polished wooden backboard with a glass plaque engraved with her name and details.

After the arrival of his first son (me) my father worked out that he could carve the other half to make a complete boat. This he did, so well that you cannot tell which half is the original! When she went for her 'ocean' trials (in the family bath) she listed heavily, because the two woods were of different densities. My father drilled into the light side and inserted lead until she floated level, he then plugged the hole. Between us we added masts and rigging. This has deteriorated over the years, but I still have the hulk.

The time was the early 30's and my father was just a lowly clerk, my mother had typically become a housewife on the birth of my older sister. In these lean times our summer holidays were rather austere, so they were spent in a bungalow on the canal bank. One of my father's jobs as an accountant was to collect the rents from the warehouses in the docks; this also included the ground rents for the bungalows on the canal banks. He became friendly with two tenants who owned one, and they very kindly let us use it during the holidays. It was called Hyltonia as it had been built by a couple called Hylda and Tony. The current owners were Harry Cole and Chris Hewlett, who worked together at the gasworks in Bristol Road (now abandoned). Harry and Chris used to join us at weekends for swimming and fishing. They travelled on Harrys' 500 cc. Panther motorcycle, which he was able to ride along the towpath and right up to the front door.

14

Enjoying the sun with my mother and sister at 'Hyltonia'.

They were hard workingmen, who lived in Hartington Road. Chris had an unusual expression, which I have never heard anyone else use. I suppose that it was his gentle way of swearing. He used to say, "Well, blues me!" I assume that 'blues' was symbolic of the use of a blue pencil to censor a swearword.

Starting from Sellars Bridge, Hyltonia was the fourth bungalow along the towpath towards Gloucester, and was the first which was level with the towpath. It had a long sloping lawn at the front, but this was excavated years later when an oil depot was built opposite and the barges needed to turn round to save travelling all the way up into the docks. This however was not the demise of Hyltonia. It was commandeered by the War Department to provide essential worker accommodation at 7 M.U. (Maintenance Unit), Quedgeley.

Resting in my mother's arms while she sits on an operating arm of the Sellars Bridge.

My father and Harry Cole enjoying our diving raft.

With my father and sister who are standing in the
lay-by dug into the canal bank.

We never stayed there again, because after the war the occupiers refused to leave. Instead it got burnt down and the family were rehoused; a sad end, but the memories of our time there are all good! Harry, Chris and my dad even built an extra bedroom during our time there, as our family was growing up. There was no water or electricity and the toilet was a deep pit with a shed over it. There was a wooden seat with a hole in it, and it was hidden in a circle of bushes. A revolving sign proclaimed vacant or engaged.

Lighting was by oil lamps; water had to be carried from the bridge keeper's house, and the refrigerator was a concreted hole in the ground on the North side. It had a steel manhole cover, where food stayed fresh for days! Entertainment was a wind-up record player. The collection was quite minimal, but whenever I hear one of the songs, it brings back rosy memories. One of these was 'Ain't it grand to be blooming well dead', but the morbid implication went over our heads!

In those days we swam in the canal almost daily. This activity is totally banned today and I wonder why, as we never came to any harm. What's more the Gloucester to Sharpness canal is the reservoir for a million people in Bristol, so if they can drink it, why can't we swim in it? We had a diving raft made with planks and oil drums, and several truck inner tubes to lie on and just drift. I even learned to swim there by jumping in with a rope around my waist so that I could be pulled out if necessary.

The summer before, I had been playing on the bank with wooden homemade boats. One drifted away and I over -reached to retrieve it and fell in! There was a sort of shelf and then the side dropped straight down to the original depth, which was at least 18 feet! I was completely disorientated and started to crawl up the side! It started to get lighter, so I knew that I was going the right way. I grabbed a handful of reeds and pulled myself out. I ran up to my mother, soaking wet and muddy, for sympathy. When I told her I had nearly drowned, all she said was "Oh" in her usual placid way, but a determined effort was made to teach me to swim after that, so she must have been concerned.

Right outside our bungalow a lay-by had been dug into the bank. It was almost 50 feet long and 10 feet wide. It was probably about 3 feet deep, and it had been made to accommodate the bank maintenance crews' barge while they were in the area. The edges of the lay-by were retained with wooden piles and thus made a very safe place in which to learn to swim, unless of course you wandered too far toward the canal, then you fell off the underwater shelf!

While the lay-by was occupied by a barge, the workers used to start work at 6a.m. By about 8:30 they were ready for their breakfast. They cleaned their shovels and cooked eggs and bacon on them over a fire. My sister and I watched, fascinated and our mouths must have been watering, because they always invited us to join them. Every time I smell eggs and bacon cooking to this day, I remember those breakfasts on the canal bank!

My father only had two weeks vacation, so he cycled home each day to pick up the papers and the mail and then on to work. He would tie the papers onto a piece of wood and give it to the next tug-master to leave the Docks for Sharpness. When they got to the bungalow, the shipmate would throw them onto the bank. One day in 1935, my father announced that we were getting a bit old for the Beano, and that a new magazine was starting the next week. My sister and I waited patiently for the first tugboat of the day, heralded by a plume of black smoke and a toot for each preceding bridge. At last it drew level and with that day's paper was a first edition of the Mickey Mouse magazine. Mickey Mouse himself was conceived in 1928, which makes him two years older than me. A copy of the Mickey Mouse magazine recently sold for £1000! (I should have kept mine!).

I can remember most of the names of the canal tugboats; Speedwell, Iris, Hazel, Mayflower, Primrose, Stanegarth and Resolute. They were steam powered, but some were later converted to diesel. The latest one to be added was called Addie and we all wondered why, because it sounded as though it was named after Adolf Hitler, who was making such a nuisance of himself in Europe. We never did find out!

Our nearest shop was Hardwicke Village Stores where we could buy provisions. We children had a surprise sweet pack for a halfpenny. In it was a sherbet fountain, some brown stuff called old man's beard and a piece of natural liquorice stick, which was tough and had to be chewed. It even contained a model aeroplane made of balsa wood which had to be self-assembled. All this was for what is now one fifth of a penny! They had no tobacco license, so I had to go to the Pilot Inn to buy five Woodbines for Harry and Chris. The landlord was Mr. Downton, who was also Chairman for the Licensed Victualler's Assn. His grandsons now run CM Downton & Sons, a very large local transport business.

Many people refer to the bridge near the pub as the Pilot Bridge, but boaters could read the true name carved along the side as SELLARS. In those days, the bridges were made of wood at the carpentry shop in the Docks. They were made of two half spans and wedges were put in the joint between them to form a firm arch for heavy vehicles. If a particularly heavily loaded steam wagon approached, then the bridge keeper had to go under the bridge and release the chains, which held four struts, and insert them into slots in the parapets to help support the extra weight.

On the approach of a boat the bridge keeper crossed over and opened the far span, the near span was opened by a 'pass man' who, on closing the bridge after the barges, had to very quickly cycle to the next bridge before the tug got there. A loaded tug travelled at about 4 miles an hour. There were 16 bridges and the canal is 16 miles long, so you can tell how fast he had to cycle. The horse drawn barges were much more leisurely, as they could pass under most bridges. The harness was unhooked at each bridge, allowing the barge to pass underneath, and the captain threw the rope to his mate on the other side, who re-fastened it. What a lovely way to move 100 tons of cargo involving two people and a bale of hay! It takes three large smelly diesel trucks to do the same thing today, and at what cost!

Running parallel to the canal is the river Severn. The canal does not actually go anywhere, it merely leaves the river at Sharpness and joins it again at The Quay in Gloucester. As pumps maintain the water level of the canal, this never alters for its whole length, including the Dock basins. The main reason for digging it was because the river Severn is so treacherous. The sand banks would alter position, and there are two tides every day. At certain phases of the moon the tide can be as high as 30 feet and produce an impressive bore. I cycled to Stonebench one day to see the bore and could not believe my eyes. Everyone had to run for their lives to get out of its path. It crashed over the road and lifted a Morris 8 touring car over the farmer's hedge and into his field. It took several of us to lift it back again. I have recounted this story to tidal experts and they say that for this to have happened, certain special conditions have to coincide. The height of the river has to produce a certain flow, not too much, and not too little; there has to be a Southwest gale force wind blowing straight up the estuary and, of course, it has to be a 30-foot spring tide. I have never seen another like it since.

During my time on the canal bank I witnessed quite a few incidents. Even though it is a man-made canal, it was not built straight. This was because some land owners held out for the highest price and the Dock Company simply dug round them. Two examples of this occur at what are known as 2-mile bend and 4-mile bend. The first is where the new swing bridge on Gloucester's latest section of its by-pass has been built. During construction, the canal was diverted, making it less of a bend, but for years it was almost a right angle.

Morelands had a barrage built on the outside of this bend. They used it as a timber pond to season the logs before they were made into matches, but after they closed, it disintegrated leaving a shallow muddy bay. When the oil depot was first built at Hardwicke, the tankers used to discharge the fuel from their forward tanks first, and then travel up to the 2-mile bend. Here they deliberately rammed the bank where the old log pond was. The captain then steered hard to starboard and increased speed so that the stern swung round in an arc. As soon as it was facing the other way they reversed and dragged the bow off the mud bank. This operation caused many motorists to swerve in Bristol Road, due to the shock of seeing the bows of a 500 ton tanker looming over the highway! From the vantage point at my garage, which was next door to Ski tyres, I could witness this procedure. The barge never ever reached the Bristol Road, but it certainly looked as though it was going to!

A neighbour had just bought a new outboard motor for his dingy and he was on his maiden voyage near the 4-mile bend. I was the only other person in sight, but he had to impress me by doing a fast 'U' turn, just to show off. This action caused the outboard to twist off the transom. He let it go and down it went. He fetched boat hooks and grappling irons and spent all day trying to retrieve it. He was back the next day with the Dock Company's diver and his support team. They spent the whole day without success. The attempt must have been quite expensive; when they left I was still watching. He stormed up to me and accused me of diving for it overnight, but I had not! I bet that over the years that each time my picture appeared in The Citizen, he would say, "That's the bastard who stole my motor!" But if you ever read this Mr Neighbour, I assure you that I did not.

Another incident occurred in 1944 at the 4-mile bend. Now that houses adorn the area, the location is near 'The Crossing', 'Morehen Court' and 'Millers Dyke'. A tug was towing grain barges toward Gloucester and the Severn Trader was going quite fast towards Sharpness. Right on the bend, the canal was not quite wide enough and the Severn Trader rammed the grain barge 'The Harriet' head on. The timber underneath shattered and down she went. That was the end of 'The Harriet', as she had to be broken up at the site. Some people think that she is the trow that is currently beached at Purton, but that is 'The Harriett'. I dived for souvenirs at the site and removed the name plate and it definitely has only one 'T'. Fishermen gathered here for weeks after because the grain had attracted so many fish!

Another time, traffic that was going in opposite directions met at Sellars Bridge. They could not pass between the bridge buttresses at the same time, so the tug heading for Gloucester slowed down and allowed the other to pass. After this, the tug took off, but the first barge had veered across the canal. It then jammed sideways across the bridge buttresses; the tow cable whipped out of the water like a bowstring and snapped. It then slashed into the bank just where fishermen usually sit, cutting a swathe about 6 feet deep. If anyone had been there the steel cable would have chopped them in half!

An even more serious incident occurred in 1960. The 'Arkendale H' was towing the 'Wastdale H' with a load of petrol from Avonmouth. The tide swept them past the lock gates at Sharpness and they smashed into the railway bridge just upstream. They brought down two pillars and the petrol, plus a severed gas main, produced a fire of such heat that the barges were welded together! Six men died in the accident and the bridge was never repaired. It was eventually dismantled and a rather romantic rumour exists that it was reassembled as a road bridge in Chile. This is an interesting theory, but I have talked to a resident of Sharpness who witnessed its complete breakup into small pieces. It certainly ended up in various far flung parts of the world, because exporting scrap metal from Sharpness was a thriving industry at the time and remains one of the few activities that are still there today.

The 'H' in 'Arkendale H' stands for Harker. This was John Harker, who had the contract to carry petrol from Avonmouth to Gloucester. These fuel barges are now redundant, because there is a pipeline from Avonmouth to the Midlands that carries it instead. After sufficient fuel of a particular brand has been pumped, a close fitting rubber ball is inserted and the next product is pumped. This apparently is so efficient that the contamination, even between petrol and diesel, is negligible! When the stock of balls has reached the terminus, pumping is stopped and all the balls are pumped back!

Another contractor carried their own products; their barges were called the Regent King and Regent Queen and the Regent Lord and Regent Lady. It always amused me that the female always did the towing, while the male was always the dumb barge. I wonder if the wife of the company's CEO had a hand in naming her husband's boats!

I had been swimming near Sellars Bridge one day and when I went to climb out I was met with a frightening face, together with an aggressive display of teeth, glaring at me out of the bank. I ran to the bungalow to collect a spade. I dug down at the spot and discovered a skeleton, the skull of which was what I had seen! My father sent it to the Natural History Museum for identification and they reported that it was a few thousand years old and belonged to an ancestor of a species of dog. Unfortunately they voiced no further interest in it as the skeleton was incomplete.

Judging by how far the Pilot Inn and the bridge keepers' house opposite are above water level, a cutting must have had to be excavated before the canal was dug. This makes the depth of blue clay where I found the skeleton to have been over twenty feet! The actual location was at a point where the original wooden piling had rotted away allowing the wash from passing barges to erode the bank, including the parts of the skeleton which were missing.

Another lasting memory of my time on the canal bank was that another family used a holiday bungalow opposite to ours, on the green bank side. Each year the father would lead the children down the bank in single file. They had to walk because it was so narrow that their car had to be left at the Pilot. This was always a very large American car. The latest one that I remember was a De Soto. They had to be big, because each year there was an extra child tagging on behind. The father was Jack Taylor of the Llanthony Welding Works, which is the three-story factory on the right as you go down Llanthony Road. I never remember seeing Mrs.Taylor on the bank, but perhaps she was always too busy, because eventually there were eighteen children. The Indian file was never this number, as the older children went to work in sequence, so that the highest total was about eight.

I knew the grand total because one of the boys was in my class at school. He is Joe Taylor and became a detective at Gloucester Police. On the occasion that I visited their family home in Upton Lane, Hucclecote, I was impressed by what a lovely family they were. At meal times nine children would sit on benches on each side of a very large dining table, while the other nine served them.

They then changed places. After the meal a human chain passed the crockery and washed, dried and stacked it.

Jack and my father were also friends and he told me some tales of Jack's exploits. Early in the war, steel was short and Jack wanted a boat, so he cut the ends off some oil drums and flattened them out. He then shaped a boat and welded all the joints. He actually rode the Severn bore in this boat, which definitely was a test of its sea worthiness!

He was out with friends one evening and they ran out of petrol in his American car. They were a long way from a petrol station but they still had plenty of whisky left, which they poured into the tank and drove home.

Several years later, during one of my school holidays, I went to work at the Llanthony Welding works where I learned to weld. At that time they were making bedplates for pontoons, which were used in the 'D Day' landing. I must have been about 12, but the ability to weld was useful later when I was building my own Stock Cars.

I was involved in my first car crash when I was about 3 or 4 years old. I cannot remember why, but Mr. Oakhill, my father's deputy, was driving and he was taking the bridge keeper's wages to them. My mother was in the front and my sister and I were in the back. We were approaching a T-junction in the Saul area when a Finch Brother's paraffin delivery truck came round the bend and hit us across the road.

My mother sustained a small cut to her knee, but the car was well damaged. The front bumper was knocked off, and the headlamps were smashed. The Finch Brothers truck was based in Seymour Road, where they had a hardware shop. They sold everything imaginable and a selection of their wares dangled from hooks all round their truck. Consequently, there were buckets, brushes and paraffin measures littering the road. My father rescued us and later I asked how badly Mr. Oakhill's car had fared.

25

I was surprised to learn that it was repaired and back on the road the next day!

Happy times in 1934 waving to the biggest freighter to use the canal.

CHAPTER 2

CALTON ROAD SCHOOL - 1934

My grandfather's house was the first house to be built in Linden road, where it stood alone for years. It is called Wilden Villa and now it is number 264. It is next to an entrance to Ribston Hall High School. It was a farmhouse and the fields that went with it were what are now Calton Road and Ribston Hall Schools. The city was expanding southwards and my grandfather's land was compulsorily purchased for building, leaving him with a house, a stable, two horses and two carts, but no fields, so he changed vocation from farmer to haulier. Using horses and carts he started Joseph Rice & Son, who are still flourishing today with over thirty trucks and a Foden franchise.

The first house built in Linden Road where my grandparents lived.

Calton Road School was built in 1906. My mother's elder sister was educated at Linden Road School, but my mother became a first year student at Calton Road. The houses in the vicinity were built at about the same time and the roads were named from personalities of the Boer War; Calton, Lewisham, Ladysmith, Roseberry and Stanley, while the through road to the West was named King Edward's Ave, after Edward VII, who was reigning monarch at that time. There was also a Kitchener Ave, named after Earl Kitchener, who was later featured in the World War recruiting poster 'Your Country Needs You!'

My first day at Calton Road Infant School was in 1934. At this time I still had my toy horse, but the teacher took it off me, saying that I could have it back when I went home. It disappeared high in the air onto a very wide shelf. Years later when I visited the school to enrol my daughter, I asked to see this classroom. I could not believe that this same shelf over the fireplace was about 3 feet high and 6 inches wide!

Naps had to be taken during teacher's rest each afternoon on fold up beds. These were put in the playground in summer and in the school hall in bad weather. Mine had a picture of an apple on it to make sure that I had the same bed every day.

The top class at infant's school was a separate building at the back of the playground and the teacher was one of two sisters, the Misses Woodward, who taught at Calton Road. Just before Christmas I was very intent on making a seasonal lantern for my mother. All of a sudden Miss Woodward called me out to the front of the class and gave me a smacking. I asked, "What was that for?" and she replied, "You know perfectly well", but I just did not! This was the first example of being punished at school for something I had not done and this unfair punishment plagued me right through my school days. She wanted to buy each student a present on the last day before Christmas to a value not exceeding six pence. I chose a lead car (meaning a die-cast Dinky toy) and to make sure she did not think I was lisping, I repeated *lead*, not *red*!

At the party she gave out the presents and mine was a great big tin-plate *red* racing car. I must have registered my annoyance at her stupidity. She asked me what was the problem and I took this opportunity to ask her why I had been smacked a few days earlier. She said that she could not remember, so I thrust the car back at her and said "Keep it you stupid cow!"

The best selling Christmas toy in 1936 was the board game 'Monopoly'. Our friends in Calton Road had a set, and my sister and I played it over and over for two days, with the two Willis girls. We asked our parents for a set, but we were told that we had already had our presents for that year and we would have to wait till next year. To a six year old this was forever, so my sister and I made our own!

We stuck plain paper over a Ludo board, which we did not play with very often and marked out the four sides with squares. We remembered the street names, their colours and the stations and utilities, which are spaced in between. The value of each property was a natural mathematical progression from £60 to £400 between Old Kent Road and Mayfair, as was the rent to be paid which increased depending on the developments carried out to each property. The mortgage value was 50% in each case. We cut cardboard to make the title deeds and used my mothers' typewriter to add the figures. We made houses and hotels out of balsa wood and painted them green and red respectively. My father had brought home several surplus canal towpath permits, which luckily were printed on one side only. They changed colour each year and we cut these to make our bank notes so that each different denomination contrasted from the rest.

When we finished we compared it to our friend's game and were delighted to find that we had every figure correct! I still have this game and continuously amaze myself as to how a 6 year old and a 10 year old could have such memory retention, combined with mathematical logic!

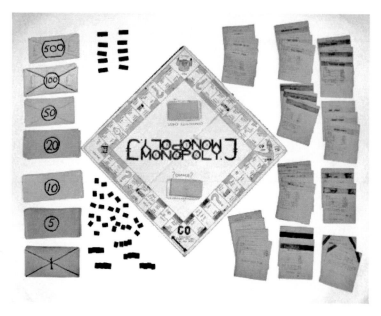

The home-made monopoly board; still able to be played on after 70 years.

I carried this mathematical skill to School certificate exam time, when one of my distinctions (over 90%) was for maths! This ability must have been hereditary because my father was an accountant. He was able to add up a column of figures in his head and had been challenged, by an office boy direct from college, to prove that he was quicker at this than by using a calculator. He won easily and his total was checked using the calculator and found to be correct! What is even more incredible is that in those days columns of figures were in pounds, shillings and pence and even in halfpennies and farthings; and he totalled this in just one sweep! There were four farthings to a penny, twelve pennies to a shilling and twenty shillings to a pound. To add to the problem, some of the rents were in guineas, which were one pound and one shilling!

One of my school pals at this time was Christopher George who lived at his grandmothers' very large house just round the corner in Stroud Road. Toys were scarce during the war, but we both had matchstick-firing field guns. We decided that a good game to play was that of opposing armies attacking each other across his lounge. We made scenery using cushions covered with sheets to give us a varied landscape.

To expand our armies, we worked out that the easiest equipment to make were tanks. They did not need wheels, just a block of wood for a body and a parallelogram shaped piece fastened to each side to represent the tracks. A turret was added with a nail with its head cut off for a gun and a cup hook screwed at the rear to enable it to tow the field guns, and we were ready for battle!

The next development was to make landing barges to enable our vehicles to cross rivers. Again these were quite easy to make. A box with one end able to pivot was all that was needed. We tried these out in the bath and they really did float, so the next improvement to our battlefield had to be a real lake. We found a tarpaulin which we tied up with string at the edges to the legs of chairs. We then built up the banks with cushions covered with sheets and filled our lake with about 30 gallons of water.

The ensuing battle was the best we ever staged with each army taking it in turns to traverse our weapons across the lake, only to be repulsed by the enemy. A direct hit with a matchstick put that particular tank out of action so it had to be then turned upside down.

The excitement increased until one of us accidentally stepped on the edge of the lake and the string broke! We were frozen with horror as the contents flooded out onto the lounge floor. While we were attempting to stop the flow, we heard screams from downstairs. We discovered Christopher's grandmother in her armchair covered with plaster from the ceiling and water still cascading down all around her!

We were not allowed to play in the house after that so we were relegated to the garden. This was not very large so we cut our way through the hedge and expanded our area to include the railway embankment. This was the old L.M.S. line that ran parallel to Stroud Road. Thus our territory extended to left and right as far as we pleased. We decided to build a den as our headquarters, so we excavated quite a large cave into the embankment, but the vibration of passing trains kept bringing down the roof!

When the railway sleepers began to appear above us we realized that if we continued, we stood the chance of derailing a locomotive into granny's' garden, so we beat a retreat and blocked up the gap in the hedge.

I was returning to infant school after the Christmas holidays, when I noticed that the door to the boiler room was open. I was curious to see inside, but did not expect to see about three feet of water, with Mr. Sysum, the caretaker, wading through it! I asked if this was going to be a swimming pool. His reply contained a few adjectives that my young ears had not heard before, but his expression told me that it was time to leave and go to my class!

I moved up into the junior school where I was taught by Miss 'Nagger' Nash. She was a good old fashioned teacher and had the best pass rate for the eleven plus examination of any school. Our lessons were interrupted each time a girl student transgressed, because she was the teacher delegated to cane the girls, while Mr Evans, the Headmaster, punished all the boys. We held them both with great respect and I do not think that it did us any harm.

My short trip from Tweenbrook Ave to school was either by bicycle or I walked. I cannot remember any student ever being taken to school by motor car. My cycling days were my favourite, because rather than ride 18 inches from the kerb in a straight line, I would do wheelies and ride in and out of peoples front gardens and sometimes straight through their hedges. My cycle was a Robin Hood, which was the name of a product of Raleigh Cycles, but it was made to a lower specification (and was a lot cheaper). This may account for the fact that I managed to snap the handlebars off where they entered the front bracket. When this happened I had to ride one handed, until my next visit to the scrap yard. One memorable day, I was giving it so much thrust that the pedal shaft snapped off at the bottom bracket. I have never ever heard of anyone breaking one of these before or since.

On the days that I walked, which was about once a week, I would start early and call in at Denleys the bakers, (now R & R gates) and would buy a complete tray of 'dripping cakes' at a discounted rate. I made sure that I kept the sticky corner ones for myself and my sister, then I sold the rest at the proper price to other students, but my sister and I ate free, due to the discount. Quite recently I bumped into an ex-pupil and he reminded me of this enterprise, telling me how popular it had been.

My father had two very unusual pets at about this time. One was a Jackdaw, which he had found injured and rescued it. After it recovered, it used to perch on the roof of our house. When it came time for my father to cycle home from work, it used to fly to meet him and ride home on his shoulder! I thought that this was quite normal at the time, but I wonder what the neighbours thought, to see an office clerk riding along with a jackdaw on his shoulder!

The main problem that we had with Jack (the jackdaw) was his fascination for shiny things. I think that he thought he was a magpie, because he started to leave shiny objects on my window ledge. I always left my bedroom window open, as this was his access to the house. Items of jewellery started to appear, so we had to go round to the neighbours to ask if they had lost anything. It soon became common knowledge that Jack was proven to do this, so we had a constant stream of visitors asking to look through his jewellery collection.

We decided that it was time to return him to the wild, so each weekend when we went for a drive we would take him with us. Unfortunately this became his latest game. Wherever we released him, he would be back at home before we were! Perhaps he was a jackdaw, magpie, homing pigeon cross? He lived   for many years and we had lots of visitors. Surprisingly nobody seemed to mind, even a girl who was dressed up and about to go out, wearing only one earring!

His other pet was a catfish. Years later, while I was in the Philippines, I noticed a street vendor with a bunch of fish for sale. I asked what they were and when I was told that they were catfish, I said "Oh, my father used to have one of those as a pet!" This caused great amusement to the company I was in, that someone would actually have such an ugly thing as a catfish as a pet. My father kept it in a sort of glass dome, which had been used to cover a plaster statue on a grave. He turned it upside down and mounted it on a base with four pillars to support it. My sister and I used to feed it with big juicy worms and it lived for many years.

Another of his pets was a chicken, which was being attacked by the rest of the flock. It had almost no feathers left, so my father let it out of the run to walk free in the garden. He thought that at least then it would stand a chance of survival, but would probably wander off or be eaten by a cat, but in fact it lived in the garden for many years and seemed quite happy. My father called it 'Dread Naught' after the battleship of the same name. This was because it was anything but big and powerful. It was small, weedy and its feathers never did grow back.

At this time all tradesman delivered by horse and cart. The household waste was collected by horse drawn dustcarts and the rag and bone man also collected his goods the same way. This meant that the horses left evidence of their passing in the road. It was my job each day to collect this for the garden. I was delicately involved in this operation when a bunch of rough lads, walking from White City to Linden Road School, were passing and one shouted "Why don't you pick it up with a bleeding knife and fork!" From then on, I crept out after making sure that no one was coming! The stables for the dust cart horses were at the Stroud Road end of Seymour Road and if you look at the wall surrounding Morelands Trading Estate, you will see ceramic grills at equal intervals around the wall. These were the vents and each stable had one, but the stables are long gone.

The wall surrounding Morelands' Trading Estate, which was once the back of the councils' stables. You can still see the vents today!

At break time, whenever a newish car drove past the school, a cry would go up "Streamliner!" and we all would rush to the railings to see this new 'rounded' car drive past, because before that they all looked like boxes.

One day, while I was out cycling, I was exploring the river Frome and the Stroud water canal in the Fromebridge area. At the junction of the Perryway with the A38, I was poking about in a ditch, and found a very old signpost with the finger post still attached. I scraped away the moss and weeds and was able to decipher the words. It said Frampton-on-Severn 1 ½ miles, Saul 2 1/3 miles, Arlington 5 miles and at the bottom, rather surprisingly, Newnham 6 miles! The mileages were about right, except that Newnham is probably about 18 miles away because it is on the other side of the river! There has never been a bridge. The lowest crossing was Westgate Bridge in Gloucester.

I researched this phenomenon and discovered that the Romans had laid paving on the river bed, enabling them to drive horses and carts across at low tide. I then concluded that the advent of motor vehicles brought this to an end, but that is not so. It was the shifting sand which made it difficult to use so in 1812 a ferry service was established at the same point and motor cars had not been invented yet! The road from Arlington to the river bank is still called 'The Passage' to this day. My only regret is that I have mislaid that finger post; what an interesting artefact it would have made today!

About to take the 11-Plus examination.

Having passed the 11 plus, I was offered a free choice of Grammar School and my parents chose the Crypt, mainly because my older cousins were there and I could wear their hand me down uniforms because money was tight and clothing was still rationed.

I was a bit disappointed because most of my buddies went to Sir Thomas Riches, probably for the same reason, including my elder relations on the maternal side of the family, who also went there and not to the Crypt. Anyway, I soon made new friends and thus I entered the next chapter of my life.

Schools for both Infants and Juniors in Calton Road

Enjoying the last rip to Weston before the outbreak of war.

Back row – (L-R) Granny Sheppard, Auntie Olive, Grandpa Joe, Mother
(peeping), Uncle Jack, Father
Middle row – Sister Margaret, Grandma Jim, Doug Rice.
Front row –Me, Brian Rice
Just visible bottom left is the front wing of our Standard 10

CHAPTER 3

BOMBS IN GLOUCESTER - 1939

War was declared on Sept 3rd 1939 and it seemed that the first air raid was very soon after. I was a 9 year old pupil at Calton Road Junior School, where air raid shelters had been built in spare land next door, which is now an entrance to Ribston Hall High School. On hearing the sirens, we all had to troop into the shelter. We were each given a bar of '5 boys' chocolate to pacify us and then had to wait for the 'all clear' signal. After emerging, I was quite surprised to see that the school and nearby houses were still there, because in my imagination, I had expected the area to be devastated. At that time, the enemy had the airfield at Brockworth as their target rather than a school in Calton Road!

During hostilities, there were several attempts at Gloucester Aircraft Company where jet propelled fighters were being developed. My first memory of bombing was when Cook's Garage in Montpellier was completely destroyed. The most traumatic was an attempt at the railway sidings at Horton Road. A stick of bombs landed in the Napier Street, Millbrook Street area and this is where I first saw a dead body. It was a girl in bed hanging out of her bedroom into the street, leaving me with a lifetime of that horrifying, vivid memory.

During these raids, the family crouched under the stairs as the government recommended, it being the only room with no windows, plus the added protection of a staircase above. A little later we were given a Morrison table shelter, which replaced the dining table and was made of steel. We lay on a mattress, which covered a spring lattice floor. Steel mesh was then hung on it all round the sides, while the four of us huddled together waiting for the all clear.

The loudest explosion of all was while we were still using the space under the stairs. The whole house shook and after the all clear, we looked out expecting to be the only house left standing. Everything looked normal, so I walked to the ends of the street, but still saw nothing. After breakfast, I was going to cycle around to find the crater, but I spoke to the postman, who told me that it was in Elmore Lane, which is probably all of 2 miles away! Two cottages were completely destroyed opposite the RAF No 7 Maintenance Unit. This was Herr Goering's attempt to destroy our air force, prior to a proposed invasion, but luckily he failed! The most incredible detail of that particular bomb was that the cottages were completely destroyed, but the greenhouse in the garden remained standing for several years after the war!

It was about this time during the Blitz that the government thought that it would be prudent to evacuate school children from city centres. Foster houses were sought and my parents agreed to take two boys. I cannot remember where they slept because we were a 3 bedroom semidetached and neither my sister nor I moved out of our rooms. I think that they must have slept in the parlour. They were from Birmingham. I cannot think why Gloucester would be considered safer than Birmingham, as we are geographically nearer to Germany and we already had a few bombs dropped on us! As a matter of fact two evacuees were killed when a stick of bombs landed on Painswick where they had been taken for safety!

A quirky saying at the time among Birmingham schoolboys was to add 'Copyright Reserved' at the end of every sentence. This became quite annoying to us all, especially intoned in a strong nasal Brummie accent! One of their peculiarities was that they had never tasted soft brown sugar and when they did, they liked it so much that they plastered it on everything, including the Sunday roast! Apart from that they were quite well behaved. In fact during one of our outings up to Robinswood Hill, my sister sprained her ankle, so they linked arms and cradled her all the way home!

After Hitler invaded Russia, the Luftwaffe was over-stretched having to supply their troops and the bombing of British cities diminished, which is probably why the evacuees went home before the end of the war.

Other memories of war times were of an Army truck coming down May Hill too fast and driving right through a cottage. Another is of seeing a Churchill Tank on its side in the front garden of No 222 Stroud Road. These tanks were being made at the Wagon Works and were taken to Painswick Beacon for testing. One had fallen off the transporter while negotiating St Barnabas round-about. It was the habit of the workers to name each tank and this one was called 'Leaping Lena', but it had made one leap too early!

What is now B & Q was the waste tip for the city before the war and during the hostilities it was used to store several hundred armoured cars. They were still there at the end of the war, as they never ever left England. They were scrapped, which has always made me think how wasteful most wars are.

Another example of this was the over production of Rolls Royce Merlin engines as used in the Spitfire. Dennis Smith, a friend of mine, was farming at Robinswood Hill Farm (now a country park) and to supplement his income in between farming activities, he collected these unused engines from Hayes Metals in Hempsted Lane, where he stripped them back to their component metals for recycling.

I attended an army surplus sale once and one of the items was a large quantity of horseshoe nails. I was intrigued, so with a little research I enquired how often a horse has to have its shoes replaced, plus how many nails each shoe has and how many horses the army owned. I already know how many legs they each have and so was thus able to calculate how long the nails would have lasted. The answer was 1000 years, which means that some stupid civil servant somewhere got his decimal point several digits in the wrong place during his calculations!

During the war, my father was too old for National Service, but he did join the L.D.V. (Local Defence Volunteers) and the wags soon changed this to the' Look, Duck and Vanish Brigade', so the name was altered to 'The Home Guard'. I do not think that they ever were issued with real guns. They used wooden rifles for their drill parades. However, an invading army would have still met with some resistance, as my father had several hand guns which he had taken off German prisoners in the First Great War. He and his troops set up targets in the cellar of one of the warehouses and spent Home Guard meeting night putting bullets though the heart of an effigy of Adolf Hitler.

In later years, after my sister and I had left the family home, I asked my father if he was nervous living alone in a large detached house. "Not at all" was his reply and I understood why after his demise. Under his bed was a wooden case containing a pair of German silver duelling pistols. They were both loaded and there was a spare box of ammunition. I remember that each time there was a police amnesty, he would surrender one or two guns, but the silver duelling pistols were his favourites and he kept them right to the end!

One of my classmates at school had been John Fletcher, who later ran Fletcher Sports in The Oxbode (pronounced Oxbodee, as in old English). He was very pleased to accept them and they probably ended up with someone who was legally licensed to own them.

It was my final year at Calton Road. One day John Lomas, who was a couple of years my junior, approached me at lunch time and asked if I would help his father erect an air raid shelter. I had already built one at my own family home, but ours was a Morrison Table Shelter, whereas Mr. Lomas had chosen an Anderson

Garden Shelter. The two names were derived from two of Churchill's wartime cabinet.

Just out of interest I happened to notice that a few years later Gloucester City Council re-cycled the table shelters that were named after the Home Secretary, Herbert Morrison. They were installed at each major entry into the city. The angle iron became the posts and the sheet metal table top became the sign; and they proclaimed 'Welcome to the City of Gloucester'.

Returning to the Anderson shelter, when I realized that John Lomas's siblings were all girls, I agreed to help assemble it together with a couple of friends, in the back garden of their house at number 282 Linden Road. The erection method was to excavate an area to about two feet deep, make a base and then to bolt the sections together, making a kind of Nissan hut and then shovelling the earth back over it, finishing off with the turf. The end result was a grassy dome in the garden that would probably have saved the Lomas family from everything except a direct hit. The payment for our labours was an invite to the Plaza Cinema (now Mecca Bingo), of which Mr. Lomas was the manager, to see the Marx Brothers in the film 'Go West' from the front row of the balcony, that for me was a unique experience. An usherette continuously supplied us with chocolate, again this was a special treat, as sweets had been rationed for over a year.

Luckily the shelter was never needed, as the nearest bombs to Linden Road were dropped on Napier Street, Millbrook Street and Montpellier, but the memory of munching chocolate and laughing at the Marx Brothers remains a vivid memory! John Lomas followed me later as a student of the Crypt School.

When army lorries were being delivered to their various regiments, they were sent in convoys of 100 vehicles, escorted by dispatch riders who also monitored their speed, which was 30 mph. In spite of this, the last few trucks broke down and had to be recovered, they were returned to the manufacturer for a new engine to be fitted. The problem was eventually solved by delivering them in much smaller convoys. They worked out that even though the leaders did not exceed 30 mph during the journey, that if a hold-up occurred it had a ripple effect, to such an extent that the back vehicles had to race along to catch up.

This phenomenon persists today on motorways. We have all experienced a hold-up, only to notice when we get going again that there has not been a crash, nor breakdown, or any obvious reason for stopping. Again, the reason is that if one driver becomes too close to the one in front, he brakes momentarily. This ripples back down the line, through several hundred vehicles, producing a complete stoppage. We cannot reduce the number of cars, but we can cut the top speed. It has been proven that at busy times the reduction of top speed actually means that the overall journey time is, in fact, reduced!

In wartime, other things can fall out of the sky apart from bombs. My father was on fire-watching duty one night at his place of work, now British Waterways Board. He was watching a dog fight between our fighters and the enemy's, who were escorting bombers intent on a raid. He went inside for a while, by which time our fighters had retired. The bombers were still flying over, but were now being attacked by anti-aircraft fire. As this was not as exciting as a dog fight, he went back inside. He heard a loud bang and to his horror, a large piece of shell shrapnel had crashed straight through the porch under which he had been standing!

One morning, while I was out on a cycle ride, I came across a crashed German fighter in a field. It was left abandoned, so I went across and tore off the part with the black cross painted on it. I was surprised to find how easy this was, because it was made of wood and fabric and not aluminium as our Spitfires were!

My father returned from work one day bursting with laughter. He absolutely exploded on reaching home because he had been obliged to keep a serious face all day at work. His boss, Mr.

Bruton, was a very smart man, always immaculately dressed, because that day he had come to work lisping through bare gums! He apologised to the staff, but there had been an air raid during the night and he had been sheltering under the stairs. A bomb had come straight through the roof of his house in Kenilworth Avenue. It went straight through the bed in which he had been sleeping, then through the kitchen table and buried itself in the foundations and did not explode! Unfortunately Mr. Bruton's false teeth had been in a mug on the kitchen table! Sorry Mr Schicklgruber (Hitler) but the only injury on that occasion was to Mr. Bruton's pride!

The house in Kenilworth Avenue still standing in spite the attack on September 4th 1940 by the Luftwaffe

Newsham House

The arrows indicate that part of our 'marathon'
route involving touching a chimney pot

CHAPTER 4

CRYPT SCHOOL - 1941

In 1941, I was eleven years old and had just joined Form 2A at Friar's Orchard. Eleven was the same age as Richmal Crompton's fictitious character William Brown of the 'Just William' stories. A small group of us of similar temperament got together and our antics started where Just William's left off.

One of our gang was Richard Brown. By coincidence he had the same surname as Just William. He lived at Newsham House in Stroud Road, which is now Pine Tree Court, an old peoples' home. His paternal grandfather was Dicky Brown of the Gopsill Brown Trading Co., who supplied sacks to the Gloucester Docks, while his maternal grandfather was Sammy Moreland, who was famous for manufacturing England's Glory Matches. This was a great financial asset to our gang because Mr. Moreland gave us sixpence for every joke we thought up and was used on the back of the matchboxes. At the time this princely sum represented two weeks normal pocket money.

Richard's birthday present that year was of complete fascination to all of us, in the form of a stop-watch. Our fertile minds then invented ways of introducing this remarkable instrument into our games. One idea was to stage a marathon course and see who could complete it in the fastest time. The starting point was with one hand on the front gate in Stroud Road. We then had to sprint down the drive across the front lawn, up the drainpipe, across the roof, touch a chimney pot, slither down a pipe at the back and run across the back lawn. Then it was to spin the revolving summer house one complete turn and proceed through the vegetable garden to the lower paddock where the old sow lived. We had to mount her and ride her once round the paddock. We all had several attempts at this and each weekend revelled in the challenge of beating the previous week's best time.

To give some idea of the geography of this marathon, the back lawn is now Firwood Drive, the vegetable garden is now Beechwood Grove and Cedarwood Drive, where the residents tell me that the garden soil is excellent and finally the paddock reached right down to the railway line and is now Tintern Road and Birchwood Fields. That was the size of the property of The Newsham House. Rather surprisingly, none of us ever got injured apart from bruises. Mind you our clothes probably suffered but 11 year old boys do not notice that!

Whenever Richard's parents went out, his older sister, who was about 14 years old, would hop in the Gopsill Brown Bedford pick-up truck and we would all jump in the back and speed down to St Barnabas Church and back singing and waving all the way.

Richard's parents were very tolerant and seemed to encourage our exploits. On the other hand, Mr Brown was quite upset one day when we broke the plate glass French window on the back lawn with a cricket ball, and it had to be boarded up until the end of the war. After that he banned cricket matches on the back lawn in case we put his lounge into complete darkness!

I would love to know what became of Richard and the rest of the gang, because I am sure that we have all done well for ourselves in life in comparison with some of today's youngsters, whose height of activity is pressing the tabs of a computer keyboard or talking on a mobile phone.

While still at school at Friar's Orchard, a small group of us who lived locally used to roam the farmland of Tuffley. We took great interest in the construction taking place at the end of Podsmead Road. This was just a track at the time and Cole Avenue had not yet been built.

The builders had constructed a narrow gauge railway from the foundations of the new school sloping down towards Podsmead road, where the ground was quite low-lying. The railway wagons were quite small, side-tipping ballast trucks. The engine was kept locked in a shed on a siding at weekends, but the wagons were always left in a neat coupled line at the top of the slope.

We very quickly discovered what fun it was to uncouple them one at a time and ride them to the end. There were no buffers to stop us, as the line was continuously being extended to help spread the spoil, so that the trucks just toppled off the end. The challenge for the rider was to pull the release pin at the right time so that he was tipped out sideways before the crash!

No one was ever injured and we were always amazed that the wagons were left for us every weekend, neatly lined up at the top of the slope again. We quite expected that the builders would get fed up with retrieving the wagons every Monday morning, but they never did!

The trucks were of a very robust construction and I am sure we did not damage them. I have wondered since whether our activity was vandalism or just boyish high spirits. I also hope that it was not because of us that the site was abandoned for two years. It was not restarted until we were bursting at the seams at Friar's Orchard, then it was decided to gather enough wartime resources in order to complete it, which allowed us to move to the new school in 1943.

When we first moved to this new school many of the fittings were hastily acquired and installed as a temporary measure. An example of this was the classroom doors. They were originally designed to be seven feet tall, but these would have to have been made to order and all that could be found were cheaply made standard ones at 6ft 6ins. Various form masters provided their own solutions by adding anything that was available to reduce the draught; a piece of cardboard or even a bit of sacking.

It was the format at the time for the students to visit each master's room for their particular period and my class was due for a mathematics lesson by A. L. C. Smith, who was the maths teacher, and, for that particular year, was also our form master.

The lesson was the first after the mid-morning break and should have started at 11.10. The classrooms were kept locked during break-time to ensure that all the students were outside. The discipline was for the class to line up in pairs and await the arrival of the master. Unfortunately he was a little bit late returning from the masters' common-room, while I'm also a little late and was approaching from the other way.

I suddenly had the idea of embarrassing him for his lateness by going to the head of the queue and arriving at the door just before he did. My planned charade was to try the handle, find it locked and then to look at my watch and exclaim "Oh! It has gone ten past I thought that the door would be open!" As of course it was not, I would bump into it.

The timing was perfect so that Mr. Smith was well within earshot at this point, but unfortunately my acting was a little over exuberant and I bumped the door with the energy of a front row rugby forward (which I was) and the hinge panel of the door split from end to end and the lock disintegrated, allowing the door to fall flat into the room! The whole class stepped over the wreckage, followed by Mr. Smith, who simply turned and said "Sheppard, you will return after school and repair my door!" This I did with the help of my fathers' carpentry tools and a few extra screws. I secretly think that Mr. Smith admired my little demonstration against his lateness, because that was all the punishment I received on that occasion!

During the summer of 1944, the Head Master D.G. Williams took a term-time vacation, leaving Deputy Head 'Dan' Fletcher in command. On the first Monday the lunch-time dinner queue was more unruly than usual (probably because everyone knew that the headmaster was absent).

Reaction was swift and the next morning a notice was circulated through the whole school, to the effect that each boy in the dinner queue must stand at least one yard apart. It was signed by 'Dan' Fletcher. I thought that this showed that the Deputy was overstepping his temporary position, so at break time, I gathered together the acknowledged 'ringleader' of each class and instructed them to suspend all other activities, such as football, etc., and as soon as the dinner bell was rung, to go straight away and join the queue. They all did an excellent mustering job with their classes and as the bell sounded, nearly 400 boys gathered in the dining hall.

As it was difficult to measure one yard, I got them to stand at least six yards apart, thus the queue very soon stretched the length of the passage and out into the playground. I then mounted my bicycle and supervised the line down the drive and out into Podsmead Road. I kept riding up and down making sure that there were no weak links. 400 x 6 yards is nearly two miles long, consequently the length of claret-clad school boys stretched right along Podsmead Road, across Tuffley Avenue and into Wilton Road, much to the amazement of all residents and travellers en-route!

On my final marshalling run I checked that no one was closing up along the way, parked my bike at the shed and continued up the drive on foot. I was walking backwards pushing the nervous ones apart encouraging them with phrases such as "we'll show him" and "who does he think he is?" but as I reached the door to the school a hand came down on my shoulder and spun me around and a voice said "I thought it must be you Sheppard, see me in the Gym after lunch!". I did, and we both donned boxing gloves. I got quite a thrashing from a man who must have been 40 years my senior!

To give him his due, the 'one yard rule' was rescinded the next day, so you may take your choice as to whom you think won the power contest. I myself counted it as a draw!

I had become a member of the Crypt School Troop of the Boy Scouts. My Patrol Leader, named Little, was a few years older than me. One day he asked me to stay on after the meeting to show me some knots. Unfortunately, sheep-shanks were the last thing on his mind. He held me then kissed me and I managed to wriggle free and escape! What that experience served to do was to confirm beyond all doubt that my own amorous feelings were purely heterosexual!

The Scoutmaster was Mr. Siggee who lived in a very interesting moated farm house at Haresfield. At our first camp we made a rope bridge across the moat and cooked lumps of rather tasteless dough over the campfire. Mr Siggee gave us a woodcraft lesson which concluded with a felling axe demonstration. He placed a matchstick on a tree stump and to the admiration of the gathered troop he split it with one swing of the axe. This so inspired me that I took the axe off him, also made one swing, and to everyone's amazement, including mine, I split the half match in two again! Poor Mr Siggee was well upstaged, while I was the hero of the camp for the rest of our stay. I should add that I have never done anything like it before or since.

I hope the tale that I am about to tell will not be emulated by any of today's students! The circumstances are different since wartime Britain, so my story can be told now that the details which made it possible have changed. In the 1940's the school had just moved to Podsmead. There was a chemistry laboratory, but equipment was in very short supply so that when the long-suffering chemistry master needed to perform an experiment it had to be done on a top bench, while the boys formed an arch round the next two benches to watch.

Mr. Smith, the chemistry master, was not too adept at holding the attention of 40 boys and for me I experimented by pushing a rubber hose onto my nearest gas tap and passed it up my sleeve into my mouth. I then idly rested my chin in my hand and gazed intently at the experiment that usually involved the Bunsen burner. I quickly learned that by opening my tap and blowing through the hose at the same time I could eventually control the flame on Mr. Smith's burner. From here on I spent many a happy chemistry lesson reducing Mr. Smith's flame so that he turned it up, whereupon I would let the air out and the flame would roar. I could even extinguish his flame completely; he would then smell gas and rush across to re-light the Bunsen burner.

I was never caught, and as far as I know Mr. Smith never worked out why his experiments always went wrong. I must have got the gist of the experiment because I attained a credit in Chemistry in the school certificate examination and only hope, in retrospect, that my disruptive activities did not adversely affect any of the other students' careers! Mr. Smith left in1948 and I assume that today's experiments are conducted in small groups making my remote flame control system difficult to repeat!

Today there is no cycle rack in the school grounds, and the car park hosts two rows of cars each day, but in 1945 the scene was very different. The drive was flanked by a concrete and asbestos cycle rack containing between 300 and 400 cycles, while in the front of the school, there were no more than two or three cars that belonged to the more affluent masters.

Just imagine the impact of the arrival one morning of a long, sleek, black and shiny Jaguar car, cruising up the drive and parking by the front door, but the driver, who disembarked from this wonder, was not the Headmaster or a visiting Governor, or indeed any member of staff. It was, in fact, a fellow student from my own class!

The dinner break was spent in admiring this masterpiece of a vehicle. The following day I stayed at home ill, whether I was sick with a fever or sick with jealousy, I cannot recall, but I do know that on my sick bed I took pencil and paper and drew this wonderful machine from memory. I have the drawing, suitably framed, to this day. I am afraid that the passing of the years has dimmed my memory as to who the fortunate owner was. He must have been 17 at that time, which makes him about 80 now. I would love to know who this extremely lucky fellow was and what became of him, because it took me 50 years to buy my first brand new car!

Among my other drawings made at this time was of my grandmother and was drawn from life. It was hung for a while in the art room at school. I recall that my cousins were amazed to see their grandmother exhibited in this way. Her name was Jemima and she was married to Joseph Rice, the founder of the transportation firm of that name, and whose trucks can be seen all over the country operating from their base in Hempsted.

Jaguar 1945

DRAWN IN BED FROM MEMORY

My drawing from memory of the car that turned up at school one day.

My drawing of Granny 'Jim', who was Jemima Rice.

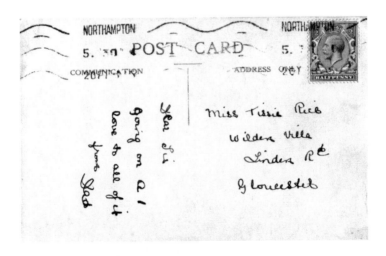

Postcard from Army Camp in 1914 addressed to 'Tissie' my mothers' pet name. Wilden Villa does not yet have a number.

Quarter Master Sergeant Joseph Rice, my maternal grandfather.

Me making an unorthodox visit to my old school.

CHAPTER 5

BOATS AND HORSES - 1942

As a teenager, it seemed to be ages waiting for my sixteenth birthday, which would enable me to have my first motorcycle. My travelling until then was restricted to cycling everywhere. For longer trips I used to walk to the city limits and thumb a lift. Instead of asking for a destination from anyone who stopped, I would ask how far they were going. Whatever their reply I said OK and got in. I made Cardiff to the West one time, and Shepton Mallet to the South. Each time I managed to hitch back home. Imagine an eleven, twelve or thirteen year old doing that today!

Sunning myself on top of my boathouse in Bristol Road

However, I still felt the need to expand my activities further, so I decided that my only other choice for now was to obtain a boat. These were not readily available during wartime, so I got some plans and built my own.

I acquired some spruce boards, which I had cut into stringers in the carpentry shop at the docks, where my father was the company accountant. I then found a roll of jute canvas to skin it with, and proceeded to make the ribs out of scraps of wood in the garden shed. This shed was not big enough for the final assembly, so this had to be done in my bedroom! The kayak that I was building was eighteen feet long, whereas my bedroom was probably 10 x 12 feet, so it had to be assembled diagonally. I slept in one corner during construction, and when it was finished passed it out through the bedroom window onto the shed roof, and then onto the back lawn. A few friends and I carried it to the canal, where it was launched and named Osprey, after a sea eagle. I had already built a boathouse next to a dry dock, which are now the premises of R & D Marine in Bristol Road.

Out of interest, on the canal bank at this point there are some concrete buttresses. This is the site that was used for building concrete barges. These were designed due to the shortage of steel in wartime. I witnessed the launching of one of these barges. They were jacked into the water sideways. I was on the far bank at the time and we were all soaked by several hundred gallons of water, that went over the hedge into what is now the car boot sale site. The last remaining example of these barges is preserved at the National Waterways Museum to this day.

This kayak gave many hours of muscle building activity, and also made me very popular with fellow students at school, because I was able to paddle up into Gloucester Docks and by lifting the tarpaulin on the barges, was able to help myself to monkey nuts, or better still, a large lump of chocolate 'crumb' that was being carried for delivery to Cadburys. The night watchman would be walking up and down the wharf, but never gave a thought to the possibility of someone helping himself from the waterside!

The other things that I acquired using my boat served me in good stead later on. There was a wartime ordnance depot, about where some houses are now built between Hempstead Bridge and the Docks. This depot consisted of a 10 foot high barbed wire fence, with periodic watch towers for the guards. Again no one thought of entry from the water, so I was able to tie up in the bushes and wander around at will.

The war was now over, and I was about fifteen. A box of army jack knives was one acquisition of interest to a school boy. I also picked up a large coat that I folded up and used as a seat cushion.

The best find of all turned out eventually to be a packing case full of N.A.A.F.I. table knives. I looked around and found one that contained forks, and another that was filled with spoons. At the time I did not know why I could ever need this quantity of cutlery, but they proved to be very useful when I went to work at GAC, where the canteen cutlery was also ex N.A.A.F.I., and matched mine exactly! To control losses, the canteen management charged two shillings (10p) deposit for a knife, fork and spoon, which I did not rent, but after lunch I cashed in a set a day for five days a week for the whole of my apprenticeship. This boosted my wages of twenty five shillings a week, by a very nice ten shillings, and this became a very efficient way to recycle ex-army equipment!

In the early 50's a popular item of fashion was the ex-W.D. Duffle coat. When they appeared I remembered the coat that I had folded up to use as a cushion in my boat, and sure enough that is exactly what it was! I resurrected it, and proudly wore it complete with all its smart toggle fasteners. They were quite expensive to buy, so when I was asked where I got it, I said that I stripped it off a dead sailor I found floating in the canal. This was a bit naughty, but I could not say that I helped myself to it from an army ordnance depot!

One of the most adventurous trips I made with the kayak involved making a cradle, and fixing bicycle wheels to it. I made a bracket behind the saddle pillar of my bicycle to which I fastened the towing ring at the bow of the kayak. Two of us then tied our bicycles in tandem, and towed the boat to Pershore on the cradle. We then hid the boat in some reeds and cycled home, towing the cradle behind us. Early the next day we hitch-hiked back to Pershore, retrieved the boat and started to paddle down river.

On the first night, we set up camp on an island in the river. We disturbed a pair of nesting swans, who were probably surprised at the sight of the first human intruders to their sanctuary. Unfortunately they deserted, and we never saw them again. A single match to the nest gave us a lovely camp fire that night, and we were even able to draw in the remains and rekindle a good enough fire the next morning to cook one of the swan's eggs.

After our evening meal that first night, we tied our clothes into our shirts and swam ashore naked, holding the bundles above our heads. After a couple of pints at the local pub we stripped off again, and swam back to our camp.

There were some lock gates on the river, which enabled the water level to be raised, so that the motor barge Pisgah could deliver to the mill at Pershore. A fee had to be paid to rent the necessary lock handle, which was needed to operate the sluice gate. We had anticipated this, and carried an adjustable spanner, thus we were able to open the sluices as required. This operation was quite time consuming, as you had to wait for the water level to equalise each side of the lock gate before it could be opened. At one such lock the Pisgah must have recently passed downstream leaving the water level low, so I had a look at the weir over which the river was flowing beside the lock. It did not look too high, and the pebbles looked quite smooth and slippery, so I decided to paddle over the weir.

My companion, Henry Morris, and all the equipment were waiting on the tow path. Partway over there was a loud noise, and I thought that I had cracked one of the stringers. I beached the boat on the first sandbank downstream and pulled it out of the water. There did not seem to be any damage but when I opened the rear locker to inspect inside, I found that the swan's egg we were keeping for breakfast had cracked and that was the sound I had heard!

We eventually reached Gloucester, but it was a sunny day and we were quite tired by now. The flow of the river was taking us along, and we fell asleep. We floated past The Quay, and were awakened by the roar of water over the weir. We had to paddle furiously in reverse to prevent being swept over. We went back upstream and pulled the kayak out by Westgate Bridge where we left it with the rowing boat man while we collected our bikes and cradle.

In the winter of 1947 it snowed very heavily for days on end. The roads were blocked and Birdlip and the Forest of Dean were cut off. The news was telling us that the conditions were particularly bad right across Wales, which is, of course, the source of the river Severn. Then the wind suddenly changed direction and the temperature rose very rapidly, causing all that snow to melt in just twenty-four hours!

The most disastrous effect of this was that the river could not cope, and burst its banks. As a precaution the water level in the canal was lowered by two feet by opening the sluices at Sharpness, so that if the river rose above the lock gates at Gloucester further flooding would not occur along the canal. Sand bags were placed along the top of the lock gates and at its height the river just lapped them, but did not quite flow over.

I took the opportunity to explore the floods and actually launched my canoe half way down Commercial Road! I paddled along The Quay and into the yard of Hayes Metals, which was where the council offices are now. When I got to Westgate Street I felt the keel scrape on the brow of the road, but very soon entered deep water again.

I paddled past the church of Saint Mary de Lode and in through the West gate of the Cathedral. I went aground again half way across College Green, so I turned round and entered the 'open sea' which used to be Twigworth and Sandhurst! As a seventeen year old youth I found it an exciting experience.

The summer floods of 2007 were quite bad and managed to inundate the water works at Mythe and also almost drowned the electric sub-station at Alney Island, but they only flooded The Quay by one foot, whereas in 1947 it was four feet deep at this point. The water did not reach the West gate of the Cathedral on this occasion either.

During the war, we school boys could not travel anywhere. No trips abroad, not even a visit to the seaside during long school holidays. We needed to do something to relieve the boredom, so a group of us volunteered for an invitation to help with the harvest. The farm we chose was Field Farm at Longford. The northern bypass cuts through it now, but then it was a working mixed farm, so there was plenty for us to do in August. Each day our first job was to muck out the cowshed. Instead of using the straw from outside the straw stack, we pulled bales from out of the centre. Modern bales are large round and covered in plastic, but then they were mere rectangles, each one the size and shape to make them easily manoeuvrable by a farmhand armed with a pitchfork.

After a few days we had hollowed out a lovely hide-away inside the stack, but unfortunately overstayed our lunch break one day causing the farmer's son to come looking for us. We had all come to the conclusion that he was a little bit simple, which was probably why he had not been called up for National Service. On this occasion, however, he registered extreme anger, especially when he noticed that one or two of us had been smoking.

In retrospect of course, he was quite right. Striking matches in the centre of a dry straw heap could easily have cost him a year's supply of animal bedding. Even though I was not smoking (and still, a lifetime on, have never smoked) he picked on me as the instigator. This just continued a well-known pattern for me. At school, whatever happened there, it was always me who was sent to the headmaster. Whenever I was guilty, which I probably nearly always was, I would admit it, but when I was not I would look him in the eyes and say, "It was not me". I still got caned, so I have always wondered what the reward for honesty is.

I was so aggrieved by this unfair punishment that I sought revenge after one such session of being caned for something that I had not done. I went to the headmasters study the next day and asked his secretary for a new notebook. As she turned to the cupboard where they were kept I slipped the catch on one of the windows. I waited in the playing field until the lights went out, indicating that the last of the cleaners had left, and let myself in.

I broke his cane into small pieces, which gave me some satisfaction, although he acquired a new one even before the wealds on my hands had healed, but the injustice remains unhealed to this day.

Back to the straw stack, it probably was me that thought of hollowing out a den, and my punishment on that occasion was an order to start early the next day. I had no idea what he had in mind till he took me round to the stables and showed me an unbroken three-year-old stallion carthorse. "Take him to the blacksmiths for shoeing", he said. I asked "How do I do that?", and he said "You ride him there, of course". I think that he actually chose me as the boy with enough enterprise to carry out the task successfully. He lifted me on to the stallion's bare back. He told me to hold the bridle in my right hand, and a handful of mane in my left, then to tap with my heels to start. At no time did he tell me where the brakes were; he just faced me down the farm drive and out into Longford Lane!

We walked very nicely down the lane to the main road, and with a little pull on his mane we turned left at the A38 towards Gloucester. When he slowed down, I just tapped with my wellingtons, and he would rise to a trot. The rules of the road are that you ride on the left, but lead a horse on the right side of the road. We did just that, and travelled very nicely along Kingsholm Road and up Worcester Street as far as where the Black Dog Way is now. It is called that because there was a public house named after the large wooden dog which sat over the entrance in London Road.

In the yard at the back of the pub were the premises of Joe Price the blacksmith. It was still quite early and traffic in those days was very light, so I had not needed to stop at any time. We got to the back entrance of the yard and with another pull on the mane, in we went. Joe was waiting for us and took the bridle, we stopped and I slid off. So far I had really enjoyed the experience and was thinking as punishment went, it rated quite well!

Whether it was the smithy's fire or the strange surroundings I do not know, but the horse became very restive; he would not stand still or let Joe lift up a leg to make a start. Joe tried several times, but suddenly he'd had enough, and he dived his head and shoulders under the horses' belly and grabbed both legs on the far side. It was a lovely rugby tackle, and over it went onto its side. I would remind you that we are talking about a fully-grown carthorse weighing half a ton, but I should also add that Joe Price was known as Gloucester's strongest man! I was well impressed with this show of sheer strength. The horse remained down while each hoof was cleaned and shaped ready to receive its new shoe, which Joe made to order.

I was completely fascinated by the whole process, especially as the shoes were placed into position whilst still red hot and actually burned their way onto the hoof to make a snug fit. The shoe was doused in oily water to harden it, and then it was put back on the hoof, and nailed there. Each nail punctured the hoof; the bit that stuck out was twisted off with pliers and thus securely riveted. All four legs were treated while the horse lay there. When it was finished, Joe went round the other side and pushed him back to his feet. He lifted me back up, and I just had enough time to grab the bridle and mane, when he slapped him on the flank and all hell broke loose! It was the horses' first shoes and the yard was cobbled so the sound that they made in the confines of the small yard was deafening. He shot off at a gallop, twisting and bucking violently as he went. Luckily, the bridle was in my right hand, so that when we hit Worcester Street I was able to pull his head round to turn the right way for home. Also, luckily again, there was no traffic because we were still at full gallop!

This time there was no keeping to the left; it was full tilt down the centre of the road, with me just about hanging on. We went down Worcester Street and Kingsholm Road into Tewkesbury Road. We passed the Queens Head at full speed. I was desperately trying not to lose my wellingtons and the pressure I was using to prevent them falling off was probably why he was still at full speed. We shot past Longford Lane, with no chance in hell of stopping. We carried on for about two miles and I had lost both wellingtons by now, so I relaxed, and so did he. He slowed enough eventually to allow me to pull his head round, and we went back towards Gloucester.

I regained my confidence and gave him a nudge with my bare heels, but by now he must have gained a second wind because he took off again passing Longford Lane at speed. I had no bridle on the left and however hard I pulled his mane I couldn't pull his head round, so straight past we went. I panicked a bit at the thought of galloping through the city centre, which must have been getting quite busy by this time. I used the same tactics that worked before, and relaxed. He slowed up, so I pulled his head round before we got to Kingsholm Road, and off we went again the right way for home. We passed the Queens Head again, and were going reasonably well, but I was still relieved to see the farmer waiting at the end of Longford Lane. He obviously wondered where I had got to after all that time and had come to look for me. He grabbed the bridle and led me back to the farm, where I slid off the horse gratefully, back onto terra-firma. My challenge was then completed, except I then had to cycle up and down Tewkesbury Road in my bare feet to look for my wellingtons! We re-stacked the straw heap for the farmer and carried on harvesting quite efficiently as we now had an extra horse and cart to use.

There was a very sad ending to the similar efforts of a school friend of mine at this time. He was called Allan Chivers and he also volunteered to help with the harvest, but at a different farm. Sadly he slipped off the back of a tractor, fell under a plough and was killed.

Exercising my horse riding skills as a Yankee soldier in Dave Lee Travis's Video Picture Show.

CHAPTER 6

EARLY ROMANCES - 1945

My first 'Puppy love' lasted for most of my time at junior school. She lived with her mother in a very large house in Tuffley Avenue. She was Margaret Davies. I never found out where Mr. Davies was, even if I thought that the lack of a father was strange. Her other obsession besides me was her cat. In retrospect I think her love of me was only based on my ability to make things, because all she kept on about for two years was for me to build her a cat's house! I stalled for as long as I could, explaining that rabbits have hutches, and dogs have kennels, but cats do not have houses! I eventually relented and made one, but I think that the cat still spent most of its time in its favourite armchair!

We stayed in contact after leaving junior school; my last contact was a letter from a hospital, where she had obtained her first position after training as a nurse. I wrote back by return, but my letter was returned as 'not known'. I intended to try again, but next time I would address it to 'Margaret Davies, a member of staff', in case the post person at that hospital simply did not match the name. But I never did, so she remains an unrequited love!

The catalyst that provided me with my first real girlfriend was my boat. For a teenager to own his own boat in wartime was the equivalent today of owning your own yacht! We all know how bronzed bikini-clad beauties surround the millionaire's yachts! Well, she was my equivalent! So after a trip down the canal one day we returned to the boathouse, where I received my initiation into manhood!

At fifteen it was a bit late by today's standards, but I am convinced (except for liars and boasters), that I was the first in form five at the Crypt!

The acquisition of my first car enabled me to travel further (in fact eight miles), so one of my next girlfriends was a nurse at Stroud General Hospital. Whilst saying goodnight in the back seat of the old wooden framed, coach-built Rover 10 we became a little over exuberant. There was a splintering crash, and we ended up in a heap in the car park! I threw the bits into the car and drove it to work the next morning. When my fellow workers saw the damage they wanted to know all about the 'accident'. I said that I had pushed my girlfriend through the side while lovemaking. They all laughed at the 'Dick Sheppard' type joke, but if they had looked more carefully they would have seen that the timbers were broken outwards, which would be impossible in an accident!

As Gloucester virtually came to an end at Tuffley Avenue, with all of the land beyond Podsmead given over to farming, I considered myself a country boy, but one of my first girlfriends was definitely a townie. Her prestigious address was The Guildhall, Eastgate Street. It was originally the Blue Coat School, and is now Cheltenham and Gloucester plc. The reason for this being her address was that her parents were the custodians who occupied an apartment at the back. It is still there and overlooks the main post office. Several councillors and staff had keys, but it was the custodian's duty, last thing at night, and on Sundays, to turn a special key twice, which secured the back and front doors, thus preventing entry with one of the ordinary keys.

My girlfriend and I planned to return a bit late one Sunday, so her parents lent me their special key. They were asleep when we got back. I carefully double locked the door, and took the key home. The next day I spent all day profiling a copy of this key at work and returned the right key that night, after making sure, surreptitiously, that my key worked, which it did; henceforth we were able to come and go at will. Their family moved to Cheltenham later, so I had no need for my illicit key any more. I expect that the locks have been changed by now, but it would be interesting if I still had a key now that it is a bank!

One of our favourite places as a courting couple was the cellars. They were used to store the City's flags and bunting, making a pile of British flags one of the cosiest places. This was apt, as I am quite nationalistic. My eldest daughter was probably conceived right there, but there must have been a couple of 'Old Glories' in the heap, because she was born in Philadelphia and is an American!

Daylight entered the cellar through a series of grids in the pavement in Eastgate Street, which provided an interesting view up the legs of girls walking past. Clothing had been rationed for six years at this time and the purchase of one winter top coat, used up two years supply of coupons. Consequently a large proportion of girls needing new dresses had stopped buying any clothes that did not show (like underwear)!

A man who completed in motorcycle scrambling was quite a macho figure at the time and attracted the attention of lots of girls. My best conquest at this time was absolutely stunning. Her name was Julie and she was Cheltenham's beauty queen. I could not pay her too much attention during the busy racing season, but as soon as I put my scrambler away for the winter I hurried round to her house and knocked on the door. Her aunt answered, and I asked to see Julie. "She does not want to see you", I was told. "I want her to tell me that herself", I responded. She called Julie to the door, "Where have you been," she said "I never want to see you again!", and slammed the door in my face!

Some you win and some you lose; I still do not understand women! So there you are Julie, you probably made the right decision at the time, but if you would like a portrait of how gorgeous you were at sixteen, then I still have a drawing that I made at the time!

On the subject of losing girlfriends by devoting too much time to a hobby, it was stock car racing that ended my next romance. Her name was Margaret Jenkins, and we first met at the T.T. races

My drawing of the girlfriend who I lost
because I put motorcycling first.

in the Isle of Man. We were on vacation and touring Wales in the Ford V8 station wagon as described in chapter 8. I bought a newspaper and read about the introduction of stock car racing at Bristol. Crowd attendances were dwindling for speedway, and this new sport was going to be mostly staged at speedway tracks, and it promised to attract a much larger audience.

The demonstration meeting, which had been held at New Cross Stadium, had caused the whole area in that part of London to come to a complete gridlock. The whole concept of this new sport fired my imagination, so I cut short our tour and crossed the river to Bristol to attend the meeting. This inspired me so much that I took Margaret to the station, and left her, so that I could give my full attention to the acquisition and preparation of a car in time for the next race at Bristol.

By a coincidence the photograph that I have of Margaret was taken during an earlier vacation in a car and caravan, and the car was a Chevrolet convertible, but by 1954 I had sold it to George, a fellow apprentice. It is, however, the same car that features in another story later in this chapter. By yet another coincidence, this same car features in the next story.

On vacation with Margaret and my Chevvy convertible
before it became my stock car.

I seem to attract the 'Walter Mitty' syndrome in people, because I already had my boat when I became an apprentice at G.A.C, but George pestered me endlessly to sell it to him, which I eventually did. Likewise, when I turned up at work in the Chevrolet, he pestered me for that as well. On reflection it appeared to be an obsession to own something of mine, because he hardly ever used my boat, and he soon dumped the car at a garage in Cheltenham Road just because it sprang a small leak in the radiator! Mister Gillespie at the garage told me that he never even called back to see what was wrong with it!

This total neglect, however, worked well for me, because it was my need to acquire a large horsepower car that made me ask him what he had done with it, and when he eventually admitted that he had dumped it at Gillespies' garage. I was thus able to rescue it, and it became my first stock car. I named it Calamity Jane after the girlfriend that I had picked up in the same car in Eastern Avenue several months earlier.

Another Walter Mitty type situation, where someone is determined to possess something of mine, occurred at about the same time that I started the MotoCyclons stunt show. It was just after our last show of the year, when we decided to have an end of season party. We chose the Swan and Falcon in Longsmith Street as it was about the liveliest pub in town at the time. The next morning I was telling my chief mechanic at the garage what a good time we had in the company of a group of local girls, and he took such an interest that I suggested that he joined us the next time we went there.

The Swan and Falcon was quite a wild venue at this time, and was known locally as the Bomb and Dagger. It even had an indoor shooting range where I had honed my rifle skills as a member of the sea cadets. Their headquarters were just a step away in Commercial Road, and shooting was one of the cadets' activities.

On our return visit the same group of girls were already there, so I grabbed the first one I came to and embraced her. My mechanic assumed that this was the one that I had been with on our earlier visit and, as usual, he wanted a piece of my cake, so he proceeded to make a strong play for her. This continued for weeks. He eventually married her and raised a family. Meanwhile I continued my friendship in peace with the girl I had originally chosen!

The Swan and Falcon was demolished and is now a rather boring multi-story car park. The most intriguing feature of it was the later addition of a road bridge spanning Southgate Street, very similar to the one that spans Eastgate Street. This one is still there, but it can no longer be used by cars because there is a steel tube across it that is permanently locked. This leaves a pedestrian bridge, and a radio station! The one in Southgate Street, however, was demolished even before the concrete had fully matured, thus were produced two more 'white elephants' to join the herd that occupies the basement of the Northern warehouse in the docks.

An example of how useful a car is to pull a girl, occurred one night when I was visiting Rees and Dave Lewis's workshop at Barnwood round-a-bout. It actually stood where the A 417 now joins the round-a-bout. They used to do odd bits of welding for me and on this occasion we had worked quite late. Our attention was drawn to a lonely cyclist pushing her bike round the round-a-bout. In those days if your cycle lamps did not work, you walked in case a policeman caught you, whereas today it is rare to see a cycle after dark with any lights at all!

What really drew our attention to this girl was that she could have taken a short cut into Eastern Avenue, but instead, she wheeled her bicycle all the way round the round-a-bout! I was about to leave the brothers, so we said our goodnights and I added "I will probably pick that girl up on my way home". I was driving a two-tone green Chevrolet convertible at the time. I stopped alongside her, and asked if I could help. Her response was fairly frosty, but I persevered, asking how far she was going. She replied "Southfield Road". I could feel that the brothers were still watching and my reputation was being tested, so I grabbed at a straw and asked if she knew Michael Mayo of Southfield Road.

It turned out that she lived opposite to him, so I explained that his parents used to visit our summer bungalow on the canal bank. This reassured her and she agreed to have a lift. I opened the 'dicky' seat, and inserted her cycle, and gave a jaunty wave to

Rees and Dave as she joined me in the car! Her name was Janet Seel and we still remain close friends after fifty years!

I always called her Jane and when I started Stock Car racing I named my first race car 'Calamity Jane' after her. It was a Chevrolet convertible and as it was a 'soft top' I had to construct a sort of Anderson shelter over the drivers' seat to form a roll cage. Jane's father was the design engineer of railway wagon bogies for the Wagon Works. I was under the impression that he did not really approve of me as his daughters' boyfriend, but rather surprisingly he actually made a very lifelike model of Calamity Jane based on a Dinky toy of an Austin 'Atlantic'.

The model that Jane's father made for me.

The end result was very impressive, as you can see by the photograph of Calamity Jane on page 91.

Janet Seel happy to sign herself 'Calamity Jane'

My father's sister married and moved to Adderbury. They had one son and two daughters. When any of them came to stay with their granny in Knowles Road I would spend time with them.

My fiancée of one day. Cousin Christine, Uncle Reg,
Auntie Doris and Cousin Audrey.

The eldest girl was Christine and we got on very well together.

This reached a climax one Sunday night, when we decided to become engaged. She went back to Adderbury the next day, and I stopped and reflected on what we had done. I thought of the problems that could occur when cousins marry, plus whatever the family would say! So I sat down and wrote to her. I said what I had been thinking about and perhaps it was not such a good idea! I ended by saying "What would Auntie Doris say?", and posted it. The very next day I had a letter from Christine, which was almost word for word the same as mine, except that it ended by saying "What would auntie 'T' say?" I was off the hook on that one, but it just goes to show how similar genes can be in cousins!

We were booked to do a show at Sittingbourne, The display went well, and afterwards the team joined in with the carnival atmosphere in the company of some local girls. Many years after, I was extremely annoyed when the agent who had obtained the booking, told me with a grin that he had been contacted by a girl from Sittingbourne, who had asked for my address. He told me that he had replied, saying that I had emigrated to New Zealand, leaving no forwarding address. This was quite true of two other team members, Gene Mace and Roger Smith, but not true of me.

I have never asked anyone to lie on my behalf and I have never failed to accept my responsibilities. I have never hidden from anyone and my name and address have always been in the telephone book for anyone to see! I suppose that, ethically speaking, an agent's duty is to his artist and not to one customer at one show, but I wish that he had asked me what I wanted him to do!

I was at my workshop in Severn Road one day with a girlfriend, when another girlfriend unexpectedly cycled up. As the guilty party I quite expected to be lambasted, but instead they started to fight each other! As I do not know what the 'rules of combat' are in these circumstances, I decided to jump on my motorcycle and depart! I never found out how the contest ended, except that I continued to see both of them, but made sure that they never met again!

After stock car racing ended at Bristol, I had to go to my next nearest track, which was at Brandon near Coventry. I knew that I needed to make an impact during my first race in order to make sure that I would be re-invited, so I turned over their star performer twice in one race. This is normally impossible, but I found out after that his fans had jumped the barrier and pushed him back onto his wheels! His name was Wild Bill Bendix, because he looked just like the film star of that name!

After the race Charles Ochiltree asked to see me in his office, he gave me £100, and said that I could have the same for each car that I overturned in the future. I made sure that I did just that as often as I could, and at each meeting I would collect my winnings with the other drivers, and then go to Mr. Ochiltree's office to collect my bonus. Mr. Ochiltree's secretary was a very attractive lady, so I asked her out. We spent our first date in the secluded corner of a cornfield. During our time there, I was aware of fairly heavy aircraft activity, and vaguely thought that we must be on a flight path to Coventry airport. It eventually dawned on me that it was the same aircraft going round and round. The pilot was probably giving 15 minute flights showing places of local interest, and we had become one of them! The lady insisted on a hotel room after that, but that proved to be quite expensive, in spite of my bonus payments!

CHAPTER 7

MY FIRST JOB - 1947

Having matriculated for enrolment to Cambridge University, and suffered the embarrassment of going up on the stage to receive a school prize, my parents must have thought that I was heading for a prestigious career. Imagine their disappointment when I refused to go to college, but instead I had got a job in a small motorcycle repair shop.

The actual reason for receiving a prize was that in the 5th year, marks were scored based on the results of GCSE (General Certificate of Secondary Education). Normally all the non-prize winners would take no interest. Instead we played battleships at the back of the hall, but our 5th year form master, A.L.C. 'Elsie' Smith, had told us that if we passed GCSE that it would be worth £5.00 extra for the rest of our lives. This sounded good, so I swatted for 3 months and got the top marks of anyone, which just goes to show that the ability must have been there all along. However, I have no regrets whatsoever for my life. Imagine being a lawyer or accountant or something as dull as that. Instead I have enjoyed a very interesting and varied life.

So it came about that while my parents were on their summer vacation I went into town and managed to secure myself a job as a junior motor-cycle mechanic at Goddard and King, 81 Barton Street, but this is now 137 Eastgate Street because in those days Eastgate Street terminated near to the old Roman East gate at Brunswick Road, but in the 1970s it swallowed up Barton Street as far as the leisure centre. It was next door to the Chinese restaurant near to the old Victorian baths.

Brian Goddard had left before I joined, and the 'King' was the owner of the very large motorcycle distributors, Kings of Oxford. The shop was run by a King's appointed manager, a salesman, a skilled mechanic and me. The salesman was the first to leave, followed a short time later by the mechanic, leaving me to prepare the new machines for sale and to carry out all the repairs on customer's machines.

As I was the first to arrive each morning I had all the keys. One day whilst I was busy repairing motorcycles in the workshop, customers kept interrupting me by wandering into my domain, as the shop was unattended. The manager had not turned up. The next day I dragged my motorcycle repair bench into the shop and carried on working and selling the odd part in between. This continued for a while, and each payday I extracted my wages from the till and left a receipt in the drawer.

Eventually, I had a smartly dressed visitor who asked to see the manager. I said he was out at the moment, but when he asked me directly as to when I last saw him, I admitted that he had not turned up for some time. He then introduced himself as Mister King and demanded to know where all the money was. He calmed down when I showed him the till with a considerable amount of money in it, plus my receipts. He apologised, and said with regret, that the situation could not continue with a seventeen year old in sole charge of the business, and gave me a week's notice. Thus I had progressed from junior mechanic, through salesman, to office manager in about three months, only to be made redundant!

At this time my own motorcycle was a hand gear change 250 cc B.S.A., and apart from the wonderful experience, the other thing I gained from being at Goddard and King was my first real motorcycle. It was at this time that the surplus army vehicles were being auctioned at Ruddington and Mister King had successfully bid for six dispatch riders machines. We were at full strength at this time, so it fell to the mechanic and me to take the firm's pick-up to collect them.

The sales ground was a sea of mud and as junior, it was my job to wade through this and fasten a chain round six of the bikes. Even though I had just obtained a distinction in mathematics in the school certificate examination, I miss-counted (accidentally on purpose) and fastened the chain round seven bikes. A winch truck then dragged them to the edge of the field, and we piled them into the pick-up. It was a long hard day and the mechanic had promised to take his wife out, so I volunteered to drop him off at his house, then I took the truck home for the night. I selected a complete looking ex-WD 350 Ariel NG as my reward, and this was my mount for many years.

Later on when I was in sole charge of the shop, I discovered the necessary forms that were required to register a ex W.D. machine among the paperwork, so I was thus able to establish ownership of my little present from Her Majesty the Queen.

My registration was HFH 26, which caused amusement to anyone who was ex-RAF because 26 is the RAF code for 'manhandle machine' and I quite often had to push my bike out of a muddy ditch when I entered motor cycle trials a few years later!

The W.D. version of the 350 NG Ariel had a higher ground clearance than standard, and over the next few years I exchanged the cast iron fly wheels for a turned steel set. I fitted high lift cams by H.W.E. Hartley, increased the compression ratio, fitted a larger carburettor and made my motorcycle into a very potent machine indeed. Of all the ex-W.D. motorcycles, the only models that had telescopic front forks were the Matchless and the Velocette. The latter had pneumatic forks, but the Matchless was the best, as they had double action hydraulic damping.

During my next job I had access to a comprehensive workshop so I was able to have made the necessary parts to convert my old 'girder' forks to telescopic, using ones from a Matchless.

One of the other machines, that we had collected from Ruddington, turned out to be a pre-war Triumph Speed Twin. When we cleaned off the khaki paint we discovered the original maroon and chrome, which was just like new. It must have been someone's pride and joy and had been 'commandeered' for army use.

After it was cleaned and polished, I was adjusting the carburettor and in my excitement to road test it, I pushed it off the rear stand while the engine was still running. I must have knocked it into gear because it shot off the bench and crashed through a timber partition into the Chinese laundry next door.

I had to go round and ask for our motorcycle back, as it would not come back through the hole. Luckily it had suffered no damage, but I had to stay late and repair the partition. I notice that the Chinese still own No. 139 but it is a restaurant now.

Going back to the family discussion regarding my future (having been made redundant from my first job), it was finally decided that aircraft were the career of the future, so an apprenticeship at Gloucester Aircraft Company was arranged.

Enjoying a dance at British Nylon Spinners with fellow G.A.C. apprentices.

We did not anticipate the cut back in defence spending, which meant that GAC closed down a few years later. An apprenticeship at GAC consisted of spending time in each department to gain experience in all trades. These varied from de-burring little aluminium brackets to laying out a modification in the drawing office, which for security, was at a shadow factory at Bentham.

One of my experiences was to be in the machine shop under a tall hook-nosed character called Joe Bays. After drilling several thousand union nuts with twin holes across the corners of their hexagon to allow them to be fixed with locking wire after installation (boring! boring! boring!), I was moved onto other machines.

Mr. Bays later let me loose on a broaching machine. The operation involved pulling a broach hydraulically through a casting. A skilled machine setter had set all the stops on the machine, so all I had to do was attach the tool, run it through, remove the tool, run the machine back, re-attach the tool and set it off again. I quickly worked out that if I was very careful, I could send the broach back through a small aperture without disconnecting it, and by then inserting the casting, it was ready to be broached. This saved several minutes, and after a week's work I was 2 or 3 days ahead of the time allowed. 100% was the maximum bonus permitted before the rate fixers moved in to re-asses the time taken for each operation. I had already earned this, so I wandered around and chatted to other apprentices.

Utterly bored, I decided to be nice to the machine that had earned me all this money; I decided to give it a spring clean. I first loosened all the bolts on the various stops and allowed them to travel right to their limits. I then started it up and ran the hydraulic ram to its full extent. I had no idea that the stops were able to be set beyond the movement of the ram. I soon found out though, as there was a horrible grinding sound, followed by big bangs and a fountain of hydraulic fluid and then silence.

The stupid machine had smashed itself up! The formidable Mr. Bays revealed his full fury, and threw me out of the machine shop forever. The main reason for his anger was that the machine was the only one of its type that they had, and it was of German manufacture, with no possibility of repairing it until after the war.

Mr. Bays retired soon after this, and on his last day he said goodbye to everyone (except me) including the security guards at the factory gates. Over his career, he sometimes towed a trailer into work and sometimes he did not. The guards were suspicious of the trailer as it was always covered with a tonneau. Many times over the years they did random checks and looked under the cover, but the trailer was always empty. On that last day, they said "Come on Joe, we know that you were up to something even though we never caught you. What were you stealing?" "Trailers" said Joe!!

The starting time at the drawing office at Bentham was 8a.m. whereas the main factory at Brockworth was 7:15a.m., for this reason I was cycling past Brockworth just before 8 o'clock, after a welder had lit his torch to repair a hole in a fuel tank. There was a tremendous bang and the whole hangar roof shot into the air followed by an inferno. Several men were killed and the whole factory was very sombre for weeks. Apparently, the tank had not been drained and flushed out.

The last stage of my GAC apprenticeship was spent at the flight test airfield in Moreton Valence (now Blooms Garden Centre) where we were kept on flat rate with no chance of overtime for two years, because my job was involved with the flight-testing of the Gloster Javelin, but the prototype was two years late being delivered.

I spent my time working on 'parts' of my motorcycles (I wasn't allowed to take the whole bike in) and several other 'foreigners' as this activity was called. I also had the full use of a comprehensive machine and paint shop, where you could get anything done for a packet of Woodbines (a cheap brand of cigarettes sold in 5's and 10's).

I had so much time on my hands that I used to wander off round the airfield with my current girlfriend, who was employed as a flight-test analyst, but there were no flights. I did not find out till years later that our activities were followed with binoculars by fellow workers, who also had nothing to do. I even took an afternoon off on one occasion when my girlfriend and I got married at Gloucester Registry Office and then went back to work in time to clock out; thus was paid a salary whilst getting married! We raised two boys and two girls, all of them have done very well in life, no druggies, no thieves and no social security scroungers. So thanks again to the Javelin, which itself was a complete waste of effort; it never flew in anger and was scrapped soon afterwards.

Gloucester Aircraft Company at Brockworth is now Gloucester Trading Estate and Tesco's super market and they built the M5 motorway straight through the landing strip at Moreton Valence. My one regret is that the planner's allowed the two hangars beside the main road at Brockworth to be demolished. The site is still undeveloped and yet these hangars belonged to the Gloucestershire Aeroplane Company who were responsible for building the prototype of the world's first jet propelled aircraft, invented by Frank Whittle. What an interesting museum that would have made! People are not aware that the world's aircraft are mostly jet propelled due to the experimental work that was performed in those two hangars.

I was off work for a few days with a broken toe that I managed to sustain at a grass-track meeting at Elmley Castle. I took advantage of the 'break' by visiting Johnny Edwards, my friend from school, who had moved to North Wales. His older brother was a mountain guide who insisted that we do some climbing during our stay. This was probably not a very good idea because one of the basic rules of mountaineering is to maintain at least

Lucy-Anne with Susan a few months after our 'works time' wedding.

three points of contact, out of the four available, with the rock face. Unfortunately the toe is one of them!

In spite of this we managed to reach the summit of Y Tryfan with its magnificent view of Llyn Ogwen.

Our socializing one evening was a visit to Johnny's local where there was a darts match. This was to be between the English and the Welsh, but the English were one man short. I explained that I had never thrown a dart in my life, but they persuaded me to make up the numbers anyway. The game progressed with me adding unknown totals to the score at each turn.

I suddenly sensed a mounting excitement between the two teams and among the other customers of the pub.

Johnny took me aside and explained that it was my throw next and it would be possible for us to win. Apparently they needed 39 and he went on to say that a three followed by double eighteen would clinch it. He went to the board and said "Put your first dart here, pointing to two spaces which would score three and I did!

The whole room was in turmoil by now with every pair of eyes on my next throw. The English team were now showing me the narrow band where the next dart needed to land to score the final double. Up until then I had been tossing the darts anywhere on the board but I sensed the importance in this last throw and concentrated. Lady luck combined forces with my guardian angel and guided it straight into double eighteen!

The crowd gasped, my team were ecstatic but the overall glory of winning was marred by the Welsh who accused the English of importing a professional player to ensure a win.

They took the charade of our team showing me where to put the darts as a bit of over-acting to convince them that I was a novice and no amount of protests from me were accepted. The locals bought the obligatory round of drinks as losers of the game, but poor Johnny and his brother had to move to another local as they had been branded cheats!

By the year 1952, I had finished my apprenticeship and became a skilled Aeronautical Engineer but I only stayed for two more years as I anticipated the demise of GAC and left!

During this last period, I was detailed one Monday morning to select a crew to go to Sharpness to recover two drop tanks. Some customers of the Meteor had complained about its limited range, so a scheme was devised to add two lozenge shaped tanks under the wings. The pilot would use this fuel first and then jettison the tanks. The experimental flights took place over the Severn estuary and our job was to go and retrieve them.

We met the longshoreman at Sharpness, who told us that he had tethered the tanks to a post and took us out to the riverbank. There were the tanks bobbing about in about four feet of water! The tide was in! He told us that it would be low tide in about four hours time.

The 'Shant' in Sharpness

There is not much to do in Sharpness, so we made our way to the local hostelry, this being the only bright spot in town. The pub was called locally 'The Shant', but it was actually The Sharpness Hotel and is still the brightest place in what is otherwise a rather depressing town. The landlord opened up for us and we settled down to wait.

Unfortunately, we did not notice the time passing. By the time we remembered what we were supposed to be doing and returned to the river, the tanks were bobbing about again! We went home trying to concoct various excuses for our failure. The next day we returned to Sharpness at five minutes before low tide, picked up the tanks and put them on a waiting truck and we were back home within the hour!

As I have said my hobby at this time was the newly introduced sport of Stock Car racing. There was a first demonstration meeting at Easter in New Cross Stadium in London. Several French drivers had been invited along, who were used to get the sport off to a good start. The promoter was an Australian called Digger Pugh, who went on to stage races at various speedway tracks in the provinces.

The nearest to me was Knowle stadium, Bristol, where I witnessed my first race. After the meeting, interested drivers were invited to queue at the office for an interview. I joined this, but instead of excitedly chatting with each of the others, I carefully listened to the questions being asked as I passed the open window. Their main concern was whether the prospective driver could have a car ready for their next meeting to be staged in just three weeks time.

By the time it was my turn I had my story ready and after repeating my successes as a motorcycle racer, I said that I had been following the sport in France and the demonstration at New Cross and was so keen to have a go that I had been preparing a car for racing. They immediately gave me a booking for three weeks time. I did not have a car of course, so I had a very busy three weeks finding and preparing a suitable car. It turned out to be a 1937 Chevrolet to which I fitted bumpers, a roll cage, and a safety harness from a Meteor.

I actually won my first race at Knowle stadium. This was probably because I was so slow that the leaders all smashed each other up, which enabled me to drive through the wreckage and take the chequered flag. Thus inspired, I concentrated on the sport and made it my part time livelihood for fifteen years.

At about this time the Suez crisis occurred (1956) President Nasser sunk several boats and blocked the canal so that our fuel from Saudi Arabia had to travel all the way round Africa. Petrol rationing was re-introduced and Anthony Eden put six pence extra duty on each gallon of petrol. The canal has been re-opened for over fifty years now, but this tax has never been removed!

I was driving to work in a large American car at this time and my fellow workers wondered how I managed to get enough petrol. The reason I had an abundance of petrol was that to keep a good supply of cars suitable for stock car racing, I bought anything with a 30 h.p. engine or above wherever I found them. I had them lined up in a field next door to my house, which is now the Esso filling station, but then it was home to a horse.

With the registration book of each car, I was able to licence it for six months, then immediately surrender the licence and claim five months rebate. I had a motor trader's insurance policy at this time and this entitled me to drive any car I owned or was in my custody. As each car was taxed, I automatically had a full book of petrol coupons in the 30 h.p. plus group, thus had more petrol than I could possibly use at the cost of one month's R.F. licence!

A fellow worker was aware of this, so one day he recounted a problem to me. His brother was getting married in mid-Wales and guests were coming from all over England but they did not have enough petrol. This cost 3/6 d (17-1/2 p) per gallon at the time, so I made the black market price of 3/6 d per coupon.

We spent the break time haggling over how much each guest would need and eventually he nearly cleaned me out of stock. I said that I only have a few left and he had better have them as well for safety. As the deal was completed and I had no coupons left, the radio programme 'Music while you work' was playing on the factory tannoy system. The operator forgot to switch it off and a special news item interrupted the program. It was announced that petrol rationing would end at midnight! He heard this and fled at

With mechanic Rex Burdett on Calamity Jane in 'Piggy Lane', now Woods Orchard Road.

me, accusing me of knowing, which of course I did not, but I had just managed to sell a load of useless paper for over £20! He chased me all round the benches with a 10-inch warding file, but I locked myself in a toilet and survived. He calmed down and even invited me to the wedding the next weekend. This was in Tredegar and the reception went on for two days; it was held at the Tredegar Silver Band Club.

On the Sunday a few of us were getting bored with singing, dancing and drinking, so we went exploring. In an upstairs room we found all the band's instruments. We wiped the dust off and re-tensioned the drum skins and between us we all found something that we could play. The noise brought the members of the Silver Band Club up the stairs and we had to barricade the door to keep them out! We found out later that the reason they were so upset was that the band was only an excuse to have a private drinks licence on a Sunday, because Blaenau Gwent was a 'dry' county at that time.

Another project I was given was to take a gang to an R.A.F. airfield at Weston Zoyland in Somerset, to carry out some modification work to their Meteors. On our first Saturday night out we decided to go to the nearest town. Staff transport in those days was various. The pilots were given Armstrong Siddeley Hurricanes, of which we were a bit jealous, until we found out that they were supplied by our parent company and were export rejects for Australia. They were left hand drive and had failed their hot weather tests!

My works transport was an Austin A40 'Countryman'. As there were nine of us, we seated two in the front, three in the next row, and four piled into the back. Someone suggested that there was a short cut down the main runway and out of a side entrance. In spite of the load, I managed a good speed down the runway, but we must have created quite a lift because when we reached the end, I attempted to turn left onto the perimeter track and nothing happened! I quickly worked out that the front wheels were not touching the ground! I was, however, not quick enough to then realise that braking while the wheels were still turned, was not such a good idea! I can vividly remember seeing the tarmacadam rushing past my side window. Luckily it slowed down, and dropped back onto its four wheels.

The nearest town was Bridgewater. When we arrived we were surprised to find that the pubs had no furniture, and all the shop windows were boarded up! We had arrived on the night of their fireworks celebrations. As soon as it was dark, the carnival procession started. The floats were absolutely exotic. They were being towed by farm tractors, and were built on extended hay trailers. There were so many lights on the floats that each one towed its own generator.

After the procession came the fireworks. At Bridgewater these are a speciality. They make their own and they are known as Bridgewater Squids. There were so many, that after the display the roads were an inch deep in ash!

Opposite lock cornering at Brafield.

Receiving a 'Driver of the Month' award from Rochelle Lofting.

CHAPTER 8

MY FIRST MOTOR CAR - 1949

My father always cycled to work from Tweenbrook Avenue to his desk at the Gloucester Dock Company's head office. He was born in Knowles Road and he always said that his instructions to the estate agent when he sought the first matrimonial home were that it had to be the other side of the damned railway! He had worked the journey time out to the minute, but the level crossing gates when closed, made him ten minutes late - this was the old LMS line that crossed Tredworth Road near Stroud Road Garage.

However, at weekends the family motorcycle appeared. I never knew where he kept it, but its arrival was magical. It was an American Indian with a big four-cylinder engine, with swept back handlebars. Rocking pedals operated the gear change and footbrake. It had a two-seater sidecar shaped like a torpedo. My older sister sat in the back and I sat in the front. When it rained, I crawled up into the nose and I was the only one who kept dry. I was about four years old at this time and one journey I remember well was when we went to Cannop Ponds in the Forest of Dean.

We went fishing and caught some sticklebacks for the family pond. The only container we had was the now empty thermos flask, so we carried them home in that. My father told my sister to hold the top on lightly to stop the water spilling, but to take it off each time we stopped to allow air in. This was working well all the way home until we got to Gloucester. In those days before ring roads the best way through the city was straight over Gloucester Cross. There were no traffic lights or halt signs; the traffic was controlled by a policeman on point duty wearing white gloves.

He stopped us, so we children took the opportunity to inspect the fish to make sure they were still alright. When the policeman suddenly called us forward, my father let in the clutch and we shot across the road tossing the complete contents of the thermos at the policeman's feet. As we drove off, we looked back in horror as the traffic snarled up and the policeman, hands on hips, stared down at all those jumping fish!

Our first car was a Standard 10. This was a black square looking thing with artillery wheels. They were called that because they looked as though they were taken from a First World War field gun. We were told to say thank you to Granny for this car, because I guess that she had helped my father to buy it. My paternal Grandfather had passed away by now, so most weekends we had to take Granny Sheppard with us. This was not too pleasant at times, especially when Granny produced four cakes at a picnic and my sister shared them out and said "Oh, Granny, you have forgotten yourself!"

In the 1940's cars left at the side of the road at night had to face the way of the traffic and carry a white light facing forward and a red one facing back. The car's battery would not last this long so people found their own solutions to the problem. One was an oil lamp hooked through the side window. Ours was a mains bulb in a plastic holder, with two coloured lenses on a flex, fed out through the front bedroom window, then tied to a tree and hung on the side of the car. This was from Halfords in Northgate Street, who had cashed in on the demand. This night light rule was relaxed soon after, but my father had made garaging arrangements by then, as described later in this chapter.

The boxy shaped Standard 10 was an unpopular car, because Standard was the name given to anything which was manufactured during the first World War, and had been made to a minimum basic grade, which made people think that it was a poor quality product. A similar description, which was applied to such objects in the Second World War, was 'utility'. Utility furniture, utility clothing, etc. and the logo attached to each article was C.C.41 (Civilian Clothing 1941). The furniture became collector's items after the war, because although basic, it was of very good quality.

Anyhow, the Standard had to go in spite of its rather grand logo based on the British Flag. The next car was much rounder. It was a two-tone light and dark blue Singer Flying Nine that sported neat wire spoked wheels. This was the car I borrowed when I was 12 years old, while my father had to make a call at his office. I drove it all around Gloucester Docks without falling in. I had been watching him working the pedals for a few days now. Any car could be started with a screwdriver or nail file, because the ignition was switched on by a simple spade key and all cars had the same switch!

When my father returned he asked how I had enjoyed my drive. I asked how he knew; he said that he had left it facing the other way!

By the time I was seventeen, my father had inherited a rather posh Vauxhall 14 and this was the car I passed my driving test in. Soon after this I borrowed it to meet a girl in Stroud. My father had just collected the car from the paint shop where the whole left side had been re-sprayed.

I got as far as Pitchcombe when a motorcyclist came roaring out of a side turning and crashed right into the side. I leapt out and grabbed him, still shaking and bleeding. I held him against a wall and made him write a note to say that he did not stop at the junction and that when he saw me I was driving steadily along, and that it was his fault entirely. He signed it, and this note speeded up the insurance claim, but more importantly, it meant that I could carry on using the family car. This was not too much longer, because I needed one more and more, so soon decided to acquire my own.

My father's next car was a rather sporty Sunbeam Talbot 90 in black and yellow. An obvious attempt to recapture his youth! I was never allowed to drive any of his cars again, except for when I did the servicing for him. Maybe this was because it might be seen parked in an inappropriate location for a fifty four year old married man with a family – for example in Cranham Woods!

My father's solution to his car parking problem was solved by acquiring a small piece of wasteland owned by the Dock Company. It was next to the point where water is still pumped from the river into the canal in Severn Road. He joined forces with a fellow worker and between them they concreted railway irons vertically in each corner, then built the walls in timber suspended slightly above ground level. They then each had a full sized garage for their cars and when his partner moved, I took over the other garage and this became my first motorcycle repair shop.

At one time in my youth I can remember my father saying to me "I own a motor car, but the way that you carry on behaving you will never own your own car!" Maybe that was my incentive to actually smash up 2003 cars, which are my total write-offs as listed in the 1996 edition of the Guinness Book of World Records.

By now my five year apprenticeship in GAC had taken me to the flight test airfield at Moreton Valence. As the main factory at Brockworth was so near to houses, the aircraft were only allowed to take off once. All other flights were from Moreton Valence.

I travelled to work by bicycle or motorcycle at this time, but was finding the bad weather quite uncomfortable, I discussed this with my charge hand, Jimmy Cocks and he said I could have his car for fifty pounds. It became my very own first car.

It was a 1930 Rover Ten, with a very imposing looking Viking head on the radiator. It was over 20 years old and the body was coach built, which means that it was made of wood and was fabric covered. I was still a fresh air person, so I removed the hinge pins from the two front doors and replaced them with 4 inch nails, so on a fine day I simply pulled out the nails and removed the front doors completely. This was particularly useful in the summer when I used the car to tow my motorcycle trailer to scramble meetings.

My Rover 10 in summer trim (no doors) also featuring Prince
and my 350 Ariel in scrambling trim.

I called at a farm one day to pick up some bales of straw and
while I was talking to the farmer I could hear what I thought was a
farmhand cutting-up firewood with a circular saw. There was
zzzzip pause zzzzip pause zzzzip, but when I got back to my
Rover there was a goat gripping the frayed lower edge of my
fabric and ripping it off in 3 inch wide strips, and eating it, hence
zip pause zip!

I scrapped the old Rover after this and my next car was a 1937
Ford V8 woody. I paid a hundred pounds for it, which must have
been about the cost of adding the shooting brake type body to it. It
was beautifully hand crafted in oak, and was quite an acquisition
for an aircraft apprentice. However, it actually paid for itself over
the years. I recently picked up a copy of 'Memories of Hardwicke
and Quedgeley' and an article had been written by one of my
fellow apprentices. He described how a whole group of
apprentices used to crowd into Dick Sheppard's large American
shooting brake, to go to the Morning Star for lunch (Since

renamed 'Starting Gate'). For this Dick Sheppard charged 6 pence each.

My 1937 Ford V8 'Woody'.

My lunchtime customers at the 'Morning Star'.
Note whose glass has the least beer remaining.

Until I read this I had forgotten that, but I do remember that I made quite an industry of taking holiday caravans to the coast in the spring and collecting them in the autumn, as most owners did not want to leave their caravans at the seaside for the winter. This activity combined very well with my other new hobby, which was Stock Car Racing, as the season for that did not start until Easter and ended in October. I used to insist on having a key to these caravans on the excuse of checking the contents for stowage while travelling, but it also meant an overnight stay with whoever was a current girlfriend!

I was working on Gloster Meteors at this time and each time one came in for dismantling, the fuel was drained off and dumped. This was known as AVTAG (Aviation Turbine Gasoline) and was in fact low-grade petrol. The engine on my car was a side valve, low compression motor and was designed to run on pool petrol, which is about 73 octane. I made and fitted a heat exchanger between the exhaust manifold and the incoming fuel supply. This meant that as soon as it was warm it would run quite satisfactorily on AVTAG, which was free for collecting. I would drive to work after the weekend on empty, and leave at quarter to five with fuel spilling out of the filler cap! I eventually sold it for more than I had paid for it.

I was 17 when I started my apprenticeship, while all the others had started one year sooner as they had left school at 16. This meant that I was the first to have a motorcar and again the shooting brake came in handy. On Saturday nights in the winter the lads wanted to go dancing, but due to unruly behaviour in the past, we had been banned from most of the dance halls in Gloucester and Cheltenham, so we had to go all the way to the Winter Gardens at Malvern.

Being a bit of an extrovert, I always wore a top hat, and as we approached each pub en-route I would pass my hat back and each lad put a 10 shillings (50 p) note in. I would put this over the bar and ask the barman to tell us when it was spent. As we entered each bar we were met with dour looking farm workers, but by the time we left they were all singing and dancing!

There are three crossroads on the way to Malvern, and my theory was, the faster you crossed them the less chance of hitting someone. This of course is not really true, but luckily it always worked for us! Another passing round of the top hat and we were in the dance hall. To make our presence felt we took it in turns to claim that it was our birthday, which invariably got us invited onto the stage. The management either did not notice that there were only eight of us, or they thought it best to let us have our fun!

One of my next cars was a luxurious Humber Super Snipe. By now petrol was three shillings and six pence a gallon (17-1/2 p). After the decimalization of money and liquids this translates to about 2p a litre, but nevertheless it was the reason why such a large car could be bought so cheaply. The first job I did was to remove the engine and fit a Perkins P 6 unit from a Commer truck. This was a bit noisy, a bit smelly and did not have such a wide range of r.p.m. as the petrol engine, but was so cheap to run that these drawbacks were acceptable. I used to run it on unrefined paraffin, to which I added one pint of spindle oil to each gallon. I could then drive a 200 mile round trip to London for less than £1!

If anyone broke down beyond a quick repair near to my garage, I would offer to take them, their luggage, their family and their car on a trailer right back to their home, using one of my part-time employees, who relished the job. It became a very popular service, as the customers were usually returning from their holidays with no money left; it turned out to be the best solution. They had their car at home to repair at leisure. I did not have a yard full of broken down cars and my driver had strict instructions not to unload the car until the owner went round to friends or relations and then paid the bill in cash.

CHAPTER 9

MOVING HOUSE TO TUFFLEY - 1951

In 1951 my father was 53 and I had just reached the age to enable me to vote. To do this you had to be 21 then, which was changed to 18 in 1970. My father was Chief Accountant in the Western Region of British Waterways. I was receiving top pay as an Aeronautical Engineer, and my sister was managing a local insurance company office. So, as a family we decided that we should move to a better house. The top of our budget was £4000, and it was left to me to find somewhere.

My instructions were; three bedrooms, detached, greenhouse, large garden, parking for two cars, but still in the City. I soon found it! It was detached, had 4 bedrooms, a large mature garden and the bonus for me was that it had off road parking for 4 cars, brick built garages for 3 more cars and a very large workshop with 3 phase electricity! All these extras, and still within budget!

I went flying home with the good news and all my father said was "What about the greenhouse?" With the other feel-good factors, I had forgotten that there had to be a greenhouse! This was not for tomatoes or peppers or courgettes, but to accommodate my father's collection of cacti! I had never been a lover of those spiky things, especially when my father used to drag my sister and me out of bed in the middle of the night to witness one blooming! I suppose it was a marvel of nature to watch the flower open before your eyes and reach its full grandeur in such a short time. It also exuded an exotic smell. At this stage my father used the tip of the tail of my mother's fox fur to pollinate it. Out of curiosity I would sneak into his greenhouse before school the next morning to inspect the bloom again and there it was, like a piece of old rag, dead on the floor!

Anyway, it was his hobby, so I had to strike a deal. If he agreed to buy this wonderful house, I would build a greenhouse. The final

103

The last photo taken at Tweenbrook Ave dressed very typically in overalls.

The Villa as it was in 1951 with its original hawthorn hedge.

agreed price was £3995 which meant that my budget to build a greenhouse was just £5. I sold everything I could to buy the materials and scrounged the rest. In three days I had built a greenhouse and it is still there today!

On completion of the purchase the vendor called round one day with a dog called Prince. He handed me the lead and said "By the way, this dog goes with the house" and calmly walked away! The deeds of the property were very interesting. From them we learned that the strip of land bordering the Stroud Road on the East side was owned by the Church Commissioners and stretched right out to the City limits at Whaddon Green. The Deeds were dated late in the 1700's but the house was not built until 1876. They were made of parchment and the details were written with a quill pen. The seal was impressed in wax and duty was paid by the addition of a tuppenny stamp. One of the signatories was Sir Robert Raikes, the founder of the world's first Sunday school.

My father's collection of cacti in the £5 greenhouse and is still there.

Unfortunately a drug crazed neighbour broke in and stole it together with my mother's birth certificate and her wedding certificate. The latter are only pieces of paper replaceable by paying a fee to the Registry Office but the Deeds were of course, totally unique. The thief certainly contributed to my mother's early demise, because every night when I wished her goodnight, she said that she hoped that we will not be robbed again. In the morning her first question was "Were we robbed last night?" Before the robbery she was definitely fit enough to get her Royal telegram.

The thief was caught four years later while committing another robbery in Abingdon. His was the first arrest by Gloucester Police based on forensic evidence, because when he broke into The Villa, he cut himself and left his blood on a tissue from which they were able to analyse his DNA. Well done Gloucester Police, but the punishment for the devastating effect that his action had on my family, apart from the expense of having to employ a solicitor in order to re-establish the legal ownership of the property, was a mere six months probation.

The home is called The Villa in Stroud Road. It had no number then, but when house numbering was extended a few years later, it became number 389. It has remained our family home for over 50 years, which is unusual as the average family moves every 7 years. It still has a very large secluded garden, even though we sold off two building plots in Woods Orchard Road. We can also securely garage all the family cars, which is comforting in these days of mindless vandalism.

I was in the back yard one day when I noticed an old man peering over the side gate. I asked if I could help him, and he apologised most profusely, but said that he was curious to see what the house was like now, as he had been born there! I immediately invited him in and during the tour he told me that there had been no bathroom, no flush toilet and no running water. Lighting was by oil lamps, and water had to be pumped from a well. This is still there beside the house today, but is capped with concrete. The lavatory was in a separate building at the bottom of the garden. It is surprising that in just one generation the old house had gone from this, through gas lighting, to electric power and ended up with three bathrooms and four indoor toilets!

The house had some unusual features, the most remarkable of which came to light after my sister left home to get married. Her bedroom now became a dumping space for extra furniture etc., so one day I decided that we needed a guest room. The wallpaper had a crack, so I scraped it off. It was the outside wall and to my horror the bricks were loose. I started to remove the loose bricks and quite expected to see daylight! However what I did find was another wall! On closer examination I realized that although The Villa was built of 9" brickwork all round, the south facing wall had been built as an eleven inch cavity wall!

Thus I was able to take the inner wall completely away. The house did not collapse because at the point where the bedroom wall became the attic, the builder had returned to conventional 9" brickwork, but had made up the difference with a 2" layer of concrete. This acted as a lintel, and enabled me to remove the bedroom wall completely. I also chose to re-build the fireplace centrally, whereas it had been to one side before. The innovation of a cavity wall must have been unique in 1876 to such an extent that wall ties had not yet been invented, so the builder had used what looked like flattened baked bean tins, and over the years, these had rusted away, causing the wall to crack.

On retirement, but with still a flair for show business, I decided to decorate the front garden at Christmas. This started in 1992 when it was almost unknown in Britain to light up the outside of a house. Over the years the display grew bigger and more elaborate; and it became the centre of attention for family groups to see the display, which included many working models such as a fairground and a railway. The highlight for the spectators was the occasional snowstorm which was provided by a film-makers professional machine. Voluntary donations piled into a collection box. Each year the total grew to over £5000! This amount of cash, mostly in small change, weighs over half a ton and has to be taken to the bank a hundredweight at a time!

By now, The Villa became known as the 'Christmas House'. Unfortunately New Labour decided that fairy lights in the front garden presented a Health and Safety hazard, and introduced new laws, which make it very difficult for an amateur to comply with. I do not think that anyone has ever been killed by hanging decorations on their house, but I risk a fine of £5000 if I do. So no more Christmas lights in Stroud Road!

The Villa lit up for Christmas.

CHAPTER 10

SELF EMPLOYED - 1954

My last pay envelope from G.A.C. was the last salary that I ever received. It was 1954, and I was 24 years old. In conjunction with my talented stock car mechanic, Rex Burdett, I had been running a car and motorcycle repair shop from a converted cowshed in Woods Orchard Road. It was called Tuffley Motor Services. I had been running this business in parallel with my attendance at Morton Valence, but I could see the demise of G.A.C. looming, and decided to leave before it ground to a halt.

The neighbours at Tuffley were not too happy with the noise of car repairing so close to their homes and they organised a 'round robin' to have my activities terminated. I needed new premises but the ones that were ready to move into were outside my budget, so I looked at possible building sites. One of the most interesting was on the corner of Lower Tuffley Lane and Bristol Road. Two sisters were occupying a converted railway coach on the site. During the re-aligning of Lower Tuffley Lane, to improve its junction with Bristol Road, the council diverted Whaddon Brook right through their property. There was now no access to the land which had become isolated, so the sisters decided to sell it.

The asking price was £5000 and it created a lot of interest. Each prospective purchaser would first make sure that they could use it for their particular business. One wanted to build six houses, another (Mr. Say) wanted to build a depot for his coaches, but all of them were turned down, including my own enquiry to build a repair garage and filling station.

A few weeks later, on a Sunday evening I had a visitor who enquired if I was still interested in the land. I said that I could be, but why are you still working this late on a Sunday night? He replied that he was desperate because the sisters had quarrelled, and had given instructions that the land must be sold, whatever the price, by Monday morning! On hearing that, I said I will give £1000 for it, thinking that at that price it would be a good investment anyway, even if I could not build a garage on it. He said £4000 and I said £1,100. I quickly realised that he was coming down in thousands, whereas I was increasing my offer by hundreds, or less. The final figure we arrived at on that Sunday night, was £1,350! I scraped up £1000 and borrowed the rest from my parents and off he went. The best telephone call that I ever had was on that Monday morning saying that my offer had been accepted! I operated from there for 35 years and then sold it to Coombes and Ridgeon, who had been renting the forecourt for 25 years.

The site was low-lying and marshy, so the first thing that I needed to do was to raise the level with hard core. I put a notice up, 'Free tip for clean hard core' and local builders dumped their spoil there, but it was not happening fast enough for me. I enquired from friends what the answer was; they said the best way was to contract myself to the council to demolish buildings for them in the city. There was extensive post-war clearing taking place, with buildings being demolished everywhere, including some which should have been preserved, like Sir Robert Raikes first Sunday school for Girls.

My first project was a row of five cottages next to the Alms Houses in Westgate Street. I needed a tipper lorry and my ex-school friend Derrick Witting of Spoonbed Farm said that he had an old chassis/cab at his farm. This was the farm that supplied Spoonbed Dairy, which is now Dockside Superbikes, in Southgate Street, and was where my father collected our dairy products on his way home from work. The truck which he had was an ex-army long wheel base 7V Ford Thames. We cut it free from the hedge that had grown through it and we then inspected our trophy.

Meanwhile a horse walked through the gap we had made and we had to catch it and put up a fence. We took a bird's nest out of the carburettor, filled the radiator with water and added some fresh petrol to the fuel tank, splashing a little into the carburettor. We pumped up the tyres and dragged it to the top of Upton Hill. We pushed it off in gear and it turned over, eventually starting up as we passed the King's Head, which is just as well, as the road levelled out after that and we would have had to tow it back up the hill. I managed to find a tipper body, but it was from a short wheel base truck, which meant that the chassis stuck out at the back. This proved to be an asset because I was able to back across Westgate Street and punch a row of holes about a yard up the gable wall of the first cottage. This weakened it so that on the last impact the whole gable dropped neatly into the truck and I had my first load!

I continued this process at each wall between the cottages, but then there was the problem of clearing the lower part of each wall. Someone told me that the Muir Hill loader at Gloucester Foundry was only used in the mornings, so I paid the driver to track across the city and load me up each afternoon. He was very quick and I was wasting time by having to take each load to Bristol Road alone, so I sub-contracted two other tippers each afternoon. We then had one truck being loaded, while another was tipping, and one was returning ready for its next load. The site was thus cleared very quickly. I had already sold all the quarry tiles from the floor, and recycled the lead from the plumbing and the roof. I even sold one of the staircases to Wilfred Dowdeswell who had a car sales showroom across Westgate Street. It had an upper floor, but he had no access to it. We carried the staircase across the street and it fitted perfectly!

A man called at the site one day and asked if he could buy a window. It was of no use to me, so I sold it for ten shillings (50 pence). He came back the next day and wanted another. On the third day I was curious, and wondered why on earth someone would want old windows. He then admitted that the River Severn was nearer years ago, and that there had been a ship breaking business on the site and the windows were in fact ship's windows.

After inspection you could see that the vertical frames were slightly curved, to follow the side of a ship. He said he supposed that I would want more money for the rest and I said because he had been so honest, he could have all the remaining windows for a fiver.

When the site was finally cleared, I went along to the Guildhall. The contract was £25 per house and I had easily collected £125. The clerk said that there is normally a delay, so that the site could be inspected, but by coincidence this had been done that morning and he congratulated me on the tidiness of the site. All the incoming services had been carefully sealed and the Muir Hill driver had levelled the site with his bucket so we could conclude the contract straight away. I produced the £125 and he said "Oh no! We pay you!" and gave me a £125! On that day I thought of running a demolition business instead of a garage.

I carried on demolishing other properties including the New Inn at Tuffley after the Fox and Elm was opened, until I finished levelling my site. I have an interesting photograph recording a situation that had occurred for one day only. The two public

The Fox & Elm Pub with The New Inn still standing in the car park.

houses were both open for one day. The next day only the Fox and Elm opened, and I knocked down the New Inn.

The tyres on my truck were well worn so each time I parked it I made sure that the bare patches were at the bottom, so as not to attract the attention of any passing policeman. There was no minimum 3mm thread then, instead it was down to the canvas before they were changed! By this time the demolition laws were tightened and you had to have public liability insurance, so I decided that it had served my purpose and I stopped demolishing. I built Whitepost Garage instead!

This was not the end of the old Ford truck though. Richardsons of Northampton had got the contract to build an abattoir in Goodrich Avenue. The site manager was already a customer for fuel and odd bits of welding, or repairs to his equipment. He asked me one day if I knew where he could hire a site tipper. I said that I had one, but it was very scruffy, and certainly not road-legal. He said that it did not need to be. It would only be used to move soil and materials around the site. We agreed on £50 a week. As the owner I had to keep it going, so each time a tyre burst I simply went to the scrap yard and picked out another wheel with a pumped up tyre on it.

The abattoir was eventually completed and the agent came along to settle his bill. He then gave me an extra £1,200. I asked what that was for and he said "tipper hire, £50 a week for six months!" I had forgotten all about that! I patted the lorry on the bonnet and said thank you and goodbye and sold it for scrap! An interesting feature of those old Ford trucks was that the engine cowl had a bulge over the carburettor, and I was told that they were made from captured German steel helmets. It was certainly that shape, but I am not sure if that was indeed the origin.

My grandfather, Joe Rice, gave me a sound piece of advice, which I have bided by all my life. He said never buy anything that you have not got the money in your back pocket to pay for. He said if you want a house make do for a while in a shed. If you can't afford that then live in a caravan, if you haven't got sufficient for that then settle for a tent until you can, but never take on a mortgage, because if you do, you *will* have your house, but you will have paid for the house next door as well!

This policy also applies to buying items on hire purchase, but it certainly meant that I have never had a mortgage and I must thank my grandfather for his advice and helping me to avoid all the misery that goes with having one!

I approached some banks for a loan when I needed to build Whitepost Garage, but they all turned me down because I was self-employed and my income was whatever I won from stockcar racing and car dealing in the winter. Both activities, I agree, hardly justify a bank loan, so I built it out of my own hard eared income. Each time I had £10 in my pocket, I bought a thousand bricks from Graham Reeves.

As they demolished some of the hangars at G.A.C., I bid for the scrap 6 x 3 channel irons. Unfortunately by the time I went to collect them, the contractors had cut them into 6 ft lengths. This was ideal for shipping to Llanwern Iron Works. But I needed to build a garage. To this day if you visit Whitepost Garage you will see that the staunchions are 6 x 6, but are, in fact, short pieces of 6 x 3 channels welded together with all the joints staggered.

If ever an archaeologist digs up the foundations they will discover that these staunchions are sitting on Ford V8 flywheels of which I had plenty in stock from old stock cars!

I then set about my first major building project. I marked out and dug the foundations with a shovel. I then pumped water into the trench and drove in pegs, level with the surface of the water. I then pumped it out and filled the trench with concrete. This came from across the road from Readymix Concrete. I made an arrangement with the drivers to accept any surplus concrete they brought back. This worked very well. These days you have to cover the oversight in one mix, but then I simply pulled shuttering boards back after each delivery. This way the foundations were completed with a minimum of expense.

Next came my first attempt at brick laying. I got faster and faster at this, and ended up averaging a thousand bricks a day, which is as good as any professional! I must have inherited something in my genes, because my paternal grandfather was a builder. I still have an interesting artefact. It is a brass plate mounted on a hard wood backing. It proclaims 'Sheppard Builder'. I asked why there was no initial and my father admitted that it had been made like that for economy. My grandfather had hoped that my father would carry on the family business. His name was Frederick Sheppard, my father became William Frederick and they called me Richard William in the usual tradition of naming the first born son with a name taken from his father.

A legacy of grandfather's building skills still stands today at St Pauls Terrace, opposite Stroud Road Garage. There he built nine shops, and they are all still flourishing today!

The sign that my paternal grandfather had made.

So that is how I built Whitepost Garage. I got permission to have a petrol tank for my own use. I then got permission to move the pump to an island and added two more pumps, which no one from planning ever noticed. I even got permission for a second entrance, to save customers reversing into Lower Tuffley Lane, thus I ended up with a filling station, which had been turned down on my original application!

The garage now a fully functioning filling station.
Sonia serving with Valery & Lucy -Anne supervising.

I continued stock car racing at this time, but I could see that the sport had developed into a high degree of specialisation. The other drivers were importing large V8 engines from the States, and then adding extra goodies so that their winnings could not cover the expense, which turned it into a wealthy persons sport. This was very different from the original conception of Stock Car Racing, when you could smash a car up and get another one ready for the next meeting for under £50.

I took an interest in the stunt team which were performing during the interval at Long Eaton. The team leader was Gene Mace who invited me to join a motorcycle team that he was starting called the MotoCyclons. At my first appearance in 1960 I rode a bike through a plate glass window, which I enjoyed very much. After a few shows I progressed to riding a 'tunnel of fire', and because other teams were claiming to have the worlds' longest tunnel, I decided to establish an official World Record, which I did and it became my first entry in the Guinness Book of World Records in 1969.

The original Motorcycle Stunt Group in 1960. From L-R: Nigel Smith, Gene Mace, Greg Mace, Colin Scriven, Roger Smith and me.

My first attempt of smashing through a plate glass window.

Creating a World Record as depicted in the 1969 Edition of
The Guinness Book of Records.

Whilst putting on the summer stunt shows, I offered my services to Chris Lewis Plant Hire during the winter. He wanted me to dump some concrete on the river bank at Stonebench to help stop erosion. He had the contract to dispose of surplus concrete from the Dowmac factory, where they cast bridge beams and railway sleepers. He had obtained permission from Captain Francis, who lived in a house at Stonebench and which had been a pub earlier.

The first time I met Capt. Francis, he came down two steps to meet me. The third   step would have been a splash, because the river had eroded right up to his front door! During the next few winters, we have calculated that I took 400,000 tons of fresh concrete there. Today you can drive two buses side by side and still have room to spare. The current owner is so pleased with the site that he has built a large family house next to the old pub. He would like to get permission to re-build the pub, and I think that it would be a local asset, especially if it had a viewing platform for customers to view the Severn Bore.

Another load of concrete I remember well was for an old friend of mine, Fred Larkham to whom I had sold his first motorcycle years before. He met me one day and told me that he used to have the contract to dump surplus concrete. He was now in urgent need of a load, as he was renovating a house on the riverbank at Westbury. There was only a footbridge over a stream, which lay between his old house and the new one. He needed to build a bridge to allow a car to cross.

He gave me his telephone number so that I could phone him as soon as I had a good load. When this happened, I did just that and his wife answered. I said that I had a good load for Fred and she said that he was working up the bank. She seemed very cool and did not offer to call him, so I said "Do you want it or not?" She then explained that he had left her, and the house he was working on was for him and his girlfriend. She relented, however and called him, and he did want it.

He had already built the buttress on the near bank and had propped a lorry bed vertically against the far bank and needed a load of concrete dumped behind this. He had put two reject Dowmac beams across the stream, but they were on their sides. These were I-beams and are only strong if they are upright.

I made several attempts to reverse the 10-ton truck onto the beams, but slid around on the mud. Fred signalled me away and dumped 3 or 4 J.C.B. buckets full of gravel. This time I managed to drive onto the beams, and cross the stream. When the tailboard was over the far bank, I selected the power take-off and jumped out. All the concrete went into the right place, but I was more interested in watching the cracks appear under the beams! It was quite dark by now and snowing heavily. Fred was taking pictures and I told him never to let Chris Lewis see them!

120

Another load of concrete I delivered was to a farmer at Arlington. He had asked me to lay a concrete slab for his silage. While I was clearing the site, I discovered what I thought was a milestone. It simply had 318 carved on it. Again my research revealed that it was a 'perch stone'. Originally they were numbered from one and were set up one perch apart. It was the duty of each resident of Arlington to maintain the riverbank for a distance of one perch and also prevent erosion.

I tried to sell it by knocking on the door of every house in Gloucester whose number was 318. There were not many, as only long roads had a number that high. No one wanted it, so I built it into my pond as a feature. At least I had the satisfaction of knowing exactly what it was.

One of my pet hates is car alarms and intruder alarms. They are intrusive and virtually useless, unless they are of the sophisticated kind that is linked to a police station or security firm.

I heard of one specialized gang in London who roamed around listening for alarms. On hearing one, they would wait for a while to see if anyone attended and if they did not, they broke in and helped themselves to everything they wanted. If they were questioned, they simply would have said that they had responded to the alarm.

Having become too busy to run my filling station myself, I sub-let it. One day the tenant was busy fitting a burglar alarm. I voiced my displeasure and pointed out that I lived on the premises, whereas he lived in a cul de sac off Bodiam Ave, so who was the alarm for? He said that it was going to be linked to his home where it signalled before sounding at the site, giving him enough time to attend. I grudgingly accepted this, and let him carry on. Just a few days later there was this piercing "Wow wow wow" and nobody came. I challenged him, and he said that British Telecom had not yet made the connection and that it would not happen again.

A few days later there was another "Wow wow wow" in the early hours of the morning. I lost my temper and smashed it off the wall with a lump hammer. I always knew that they contained their own back-up battery, and even if you smashed it off it would not stop ringing, which, of course, it did not. I next thought that I will throw it into the canal. Then I thought what if someone saw me walking across the Bristol Road with a clanging burglar alarm? I then had a much better idea! I had been woken up, so why shouldn't he? I went round to my car and in doing so, had to circle round the caravan where Jacquie De Creed was sleeping. She remembers it well. She thought that the Martians had landed, and were surrounding her caravan!

I drove round to the tenant's house with the thing still clanging away. It was so loud that I had to open all the windows to reduce the noise. When I got to his house, I tossed it onto his roof. At the third attempt it lodged in the gutter. By now the neighbours were beginning to come out of their houses in dressing gowns to see what the noise was. As soon as I had a large enough gathering, I shouted an apology, and told them that it belonged to the man in that house and left. I could hear it all the way home, and when I woke up the next morning I could still hear it giving out its "Wow wow wow". He never replaced it and a few weeks later he moved house.

Another alarm which disturbed me was fixed to my side of Wilts Electrical two doors away, and it was just level with my bedroom window. The first time it went off I complained to the manager who himself lived at Hucclecote. I pointed out that the regulations had changed and that an alarm must switch off after 20 minutes.

A short while later, off it went again, so I pulled on a pair of trousers and drove round there in a transit van with a roof rack. By this time the police had attended and were waiting in their Panda car under the alarm. They asked if I had come to switch it off and I assured them that I indeed had, so they moved up, and I sited my

122

van under the alarm. They realized my intent when I climbed up the ladder armed with a lump hammer. They grabbed me and pulled me off the van and arrested me for attempted damage to property.

I was locked in a cell for the night and each hour they played 'good copper' 'bad copper' in turns. The good copper would ask me my name, but he had already said that I need not say anything, so I did not. Then the bad copper came and said that the next assizes were not for three weeks and that I would be held in custody until then if I did not tell him my name.

In the early hours of the morning, the good copper returned and said "Come on Dick, tell us your name, and you can go home" so he knew who I was all the time! I still did not cooperate and at dawn they let me out. I asked if they were going to take me back to where they picked me up from and they refused, expecting me to walk home. The first vehicle I saw in the car park was my transit and attached to the chassis was my 'keep-a-key' with a spare key in it, so I drove home in comfort.

I sat down for breakfast with the family, my wife and children had not noticed that I had been missing. I got no sympathy whatsoever for having spent the night in prison. There were no charges, and Wilts Electric altered their alarm, but the most annoying part of both incidents was that there had not been a break-in. Employees not shutting windows properly when they left work had set off all the alarms. That is why I do not like burglar alarms!!!

Another of my pet hates is a continuously barking dog, which does not seem to have any propose. Our next door neighbours had such a dog, which every evening after vacating their premises started to bark and kept it up all night long. I complained to them and they said that it was a guard dog and that its presence was essential to their business.

This business was that of repairing broken pop bottle crates. They had an old Bedford lorry, which was only used to deliver these boxes back to the depot. It had a bad battery and they always called on me to jump-start it. I asked how much they were paid to repair each box. When I jump-started their lorry I counted the number of boxes in each row multiplied by the number of rows and then multiplied by the number of times I started the loaded lorry. I was thus able to calculate their total income divided between the three of them and it fell short of a living wage. This made me wonder why a guard dog was needed to protect such a useless asset.

One evening the barking was particularly bad, so I went round to their premises with a bunch of keys; one of which actually fitted. I unlocked the door and then made a noise at the other end of the building to draw the dog there, I then crept back and opened the door and swung up onto the porch. The dog came bounding out barking furiously. He did not see me on the porch roof and went running up the road. I then climbed down and met the dog on equal terms and he was quite friendly. I said "walkies" and he followed me round to my car and jumped in. I took him to Bisley and let him out.

I was driving away and watching in the mirror to make sure that it did not follow me. Not looking too well where I was going, I felt a bump and noticed in the mirror that I had run over a badger. I wound down the window and called out "And there is your breakfast!" and the last thing I saw was the dog sniffing the badger.

I re-locked the neighbour's door and to this day they must wonder what happened to their guard dog which had disappeared out of locked premises! I was never annoyed by its barking again.

A few months later there was a police raid on their premises and the three partners were arrested for dealing in stolen liquors and cigarettes, which they had obtained from the nearby U.S. Air

Force base. This is apparently why they had needed a guard dog and the repairing of pop bottle crates was merely a cover up for their real activity.

I was telephoned at the garage one day and invited to drive up Tuffley Avenue to see something interesting. To my amazement the top house on the left had an aeroplane sticking out of the roof! The house belonged to Mrs. Dewey who was a member of Tuffley Townswomen's Guild, of which my mother was a founder member. Mrs. Dewey was all right, but the two aviators were hanging out of the smashed cabin and they were both dead.

The Varsity aircraft resting on Mrs. Dewey's house in Tuffley Avenue.

They were on stall-test flight from Staverton and the plane (a Vickers Varsity) failed to restart over Ribston Hall School. There had been girls in the playing fields, so the pilot almost certainly attempted to glide as far as the Crypt School playing fields but did not make it.

There was a later sequel to this incident when someone in Australia sent an advertisement for an insurance company, with a photograph of the aeroplane sticking out of the house to Mrs Dewey's son. The caption read something like; we will not make a tragedy out of an incident. We will settle our claims promptly. This upset Mr. Dewey, as he remembered that the insurance claim for his mother's house had taken four years to settle, in spite of the fact that no blame could be attached to the householder!

As a hard-working owner of a business and not being a paid employee, you are a soft target for any scam going. I was approached one day by a suited representative whose opening gambit was "Are you getting enough return from your business?" He was from an American company called 'George S. May'. My response was a rather predictable "No" whereupon he offered to provide experts in the field of accounting and garage management to show me how to increase my profits. He said that there was no charge for this service, so I agreed.

After several sessions with these two experts, when I gave them access to all my books and records, they produced me a report. All this boiled down to was a suggestion to increase my labour rate and this would increase my profit. I immediately pointed out that if I followed that advice my charges would be higher than my competitors and that I would lose business. They then produced a bill for £2000 (which represented my reserve capital at the time). I objected strongly, but then they produced the small print contained in the original contract, which said that if I read the report I would automatically have accepted it. My solicitor agreed that they were right and I had been caught, so I paid up.

It was a hard, expensive lesson, but stood me in good stead. A few months later, I had another visitor who started with the same spiel. I could not believe it when he said that he was from George S. May! I asked why he had called and all he said was that he was in the area looking for businesses that looked as though there was a potential to increase their profits. It became very obvious that he had no idea that I had already been done. They must have banked my £2000 and then torn up my records. I thought carefully and took a gamble and said "Yes!" once again. I had no clear plan, but with my earlier experience I thought that I stood a chance of retribution!

The two experts arrived in turn and poured over my books. Each day they reversed charges and phoned head office in my presence. They recounted their progress with regard to improving my business. Each day I would take an hour off for lunch. I made it clear that I wanted to be in my home for the hour, and not to be disturbed.

As soon as I was in my home, I sat by the extension phone, when I heard a click signifying that a call was being made, I picked up and recorded every word that was said. Each call they made was incriminating, but the most damning of all was: "His bank balance is healthy and I think that we can take him for at least a couple of grand!"

Towards the end of the session I was invited to visit their office suite in London, which I accepted. They occupied a complete floor in a tower block very near Trafalgar Square. The gold sign proclaimed 'George S. May' and when I entered the foyer there was a blackboard announcing that today's visitor is Dick Sheppard, Garage Proprietor from Gloucester. The receptionist was obviously an actress, overacting the part of an American 'Greeter'. She was all fingernail and eyelash extensions, and gave me a fluttering welcome. She announced my arrival and I was met by the manager, who gave me a tour of each office along the corridor.

Every door was held open by a wedge to signify the openness of each operator. Each room contained maps, graphs and a hard working executive. It was very good window-dressing, giving the impression of a well run global operation. As we reached the end of the corridor, I noticed a closed door. I took the initiative and strode forward opening it, saying "What is in here then?" It was obvious that I had overstepped my planned itinerary. My guide was immediately flustered and stammered, "It is our accounts department", but there were two rows of what were obviously telemarketers all busy on their phones.

I had all the evidence I wanted, including their report and a bill for £2,500 for the service they had provided. I phoned The People newspaper and the reporter I spoke to, Mr. Dicks, said, "George S. May? OK, yes, we have a large file on them, filled with complaints from victims!" He also said that the company had covered their activities legally and were difficult to expose as fraudulent. I told him what I had and he showed immediate extra interest. I told him that they were coming for the cheque the next morning. Mr. Dicks asked me for the name of my nearest airport and if I could pick him up from there. This was organized and when the George S. May rep. arrived, he was met by me, a reporter, a cameraman and all the recordings.

Setting a 'lap' record around the petrol pumps

There was a rapid phone call to head office and my cheque for £2,500 was ripped up. I got a cheque for £2000 instead as a refund of my earlier payment, and I received a fee from 'The People' newspaper to boot. My gamble had paid off and it has taught me a lesson. Be aware of cold callers! (George S. May ceased trading very soon after this!)

Whitepost Garage. My base and workshops for over 30 years.

The epicentre of my activities – the workbench

Two bikes through a hoop smaller than their combined width.
A speciality of the MotoCyclons

My birthplace in Tweenbrook Avenue

CHAPTER 11

PERSONAL FITNESS

When my girlfriends' family left their home at the Guildhall in Eastgate Street they moved to Prestbury where they acquired a fruit and vegetable business. My only means of transport was still just my bicycle and when I visited her I cycled to Prestbury and at the end of our evening together I would look at the time to make sure that I did not miss the last bus to Gloucester. This entailed cycling from Prestbury to the bus station in Cheltenham and waiting at the kerbside for the Gloucester bus to leave. I would then tuck in behind it making sure that I stayed within the blind spot between the driver's mirrors. The suction provided was quite considerable, even allowing me to coast for several minutes. The stoplights gave sufficient warning of when to slow down and I became quite adept at the skill and always survived the journey home! I was very aware that if ever I dropped out of the slipstream that I would be reduced to pedal power for the remainder of the journey and this after what had been a tiring evening in any event!

At a later date I took this skill to the limit when there was a proposed school trip to the Royal Shakespeare Theatre in Stratford on Avon. I was a long time raising the money for the trip and when I did my form-master, Mister Morgan-Brown, seemed to take delight in telling me that I could have a theatre ticket, but that there were no seats left on the coach and that I would have to find my own way there. I said "OK then I will just take the ticket and I will cycle there"

I was at the school when the coach party left and tucked in behind it just as I did when returning from Cheltenham. The maximum speed that a coach achieved in those days was probably about forty miles an hour, but was a very good pace indeed for a bicycle! I enjoyed the rendition of Julius Caesar which was of particular interest to me at the time because it was the chosen Shakespearean play for that year's School Certificate Examination and almost certainly helped me to obtain a credit in English Literature.

The return journey to Gloucester was just as successful, aided almost certainly by a row of fellow students crowded in the back seat giving signs of encouragement and admiration, plus the geographical fact that it is slightly downhill from Stratford to Gloucester!

My early very energetic antics on a bicycle served as a good start, while the kayaking definitely was a contributory cause of my upper body muscle building. I played rugby at school, usually as hooker and boxed for the sea cadets later on. One of the games we played during P.T. (Physical Training) in the school gymnasium was called 'British Bulldogs'.

As a rugby playing school, this game was used as a toughening up for that game. Half the class started from one end and had to pass the other half waiting in the centre. The object was to reach the far end, but if you were stopped part way you had to join the ones in the middle, thus increasing the difficulty. In an average class of forty the odds became 39 to 1 against succeeding. With flailing arms and legs, plus a butting head, I was always the last man standing!

The other thing that maintained my health was my diet. During the war the basic rations for city dwellers was minimal. In fact it was verging on starvation. For example, a week's ration each of meat and cheese was 2ozs! Imagine just how much that was! These days 8 ounces would be a very modest steak, but back then this amount represented a month's supply! In fact a person's complete week's rations could be bought for 18 shillings (90 pence).

However, my father was very enterprising. He managed to catch some pigeons at the Docks, and each evening before cycling home he used a dustpan and brush and swept up a bagful of grain which had spilled out of the suction pipes used to suck the grain out of the barges and into the warehouse.

He fed this to our pigeons, giving us an occasional pigeon pie. Rabbits were among some of the things we kept and our duty as children was to walk home at least twice a week through the school playing fields, bringing home a bag full of dandelion leaves. We also kept chickens that were fed on kitchen waste. These provided us with more meat and eggs, so that my total intake of protein was probably equal to that of a weightlifter!

Due to wartime labour shortage, my father's position as Inland Waterways' accountant took him as far north as Tardebigge on the Grand Union canal and south to the Kennet and Avon canal in Wiltshire. The territory included the Docks at Sharpness and while he was there one day an American voice from a visiting Liberty ship hailed him and asked when he had last had bacon? "Not for ages" he replied, whereupon the sailor tossed down a full side of bacon! Aunts, uncles and cousins all had bacon for several days!

These 'Liberty' ships were built from 1940 onwards at a secret dock in Boston. The builders were sworn to secrecy, but being New Englanders they were sympathetic to our predicament. President Roosevelt instigated their construction, unbeknown to Congress, because America did not enter the war until after the Japanese bombed Pearl Harbour in 1941.

The large houses in Stroud Road had been built in Victorian times, whereas our house in Tweenbrook Avenue and those in Calton Road were built in the 1920's. Each of these houses had a generous back garden, but the developers left a large rectangular area of 'No man's land' in the centre. My father and Mr. Melonie at number 10 decided that this was a waste of fertile ground. They commandeered half each and both families had a very good

133

allotment that nobody knew about! This gave us all the fresh vegetables that we needed, so that my diet was probably better then than it is now, with all the chemicals which are now added to super market food!

My father prided himself on his tomatoes, but they looked poisonous to me! My mother bribed me with sixpence to at least try one and now they are my favourite fruit (or vegetable, depending on your opinion).

My father and his friends who were visitors to our summer bungalow had permission to shoot pests at Miss Olive Lloyd Baker's estate at Hardwicke. This provided us with wild rabbit and wood pigeon. In the autumn we also gathered the biggest field mushrooms you ever saw! They were so big that they had to be cooked one at a time in our biggest frying pan!

As a man of action, needing quick results, I never have been able to sit on a canal bank and watch for a float to bob up and down, but my father had endless patience, so a feed of fresh water fish was also added to our diet. Our main garden had two apple trees, two pear trees and a large plum tree. This last tree never bore fruit, so my father allowed me to build a tree house. The very next season it was loaded with fruit and remained so for the rest of the time that we stayed there (until 1951). I built the tree house using ladders, but after it was finished, I gained access by taking a run and a giant leap and was just able to reach the lowest branch and swing myself up. For this reason my tree house was a very private place. From its lofty position it gave me a view into all the girl's bedrooms on the even side of Tweenbrook Avenue and the odd side of the lower end of Calton Road!

I weighed 175 lbs when I left school and remained the same weight until middle age spread set in. My diet at this time was the main contributory factor for this, as experts now tell us that fresh fruit and fresh vegetables, with a minimum of red meat is the ideal diet.

Maintaining the Breed

Even at 15 I had an appreciation for thoroughbred cars and horses.

The humble beginnings of what was to become
Britains' top earning motor cycle display.

EPILOGUE

A disturbing fact currently being publicised is that 33% of the world's population will contract cancer at some time during their lifetime. In my career if I had calculated that I only had a 66% chance of surviving a stunt, then I would definitely have turned it down! Unfortunately if you contract cancer the only choice you have is to succumb to it or fight it. In 2008 a lump manifested itself and it was diagnosed as grade four cancer. The best that the health service could offer was a course of chemotherapy. Having absorbed this fact the only choice anyone has is to accept it and then to be determined to fight it. My advice to anyone being given the diagnosis is to give up smoking and alcohol. Eat only non-processed fresh fruit and vegetables, and drink at least a litre of water a day. The most important advice of all is to remain positive.

If you give out the signs of being determined to beat it, then the team you have been assigned to, from the consultant right down to the nurse giving you injections, will recognise your positivity and give you the most diligent of treatment. I am not saying that every team will not do this, but I am convinced that my team recognised my positivity and were as determined as I was to beat it!

On treatment days you have to spend all day with a drip in your arm supplying each chemical in turn. In between treatments you cannot fly or take a train or bus. You must not go to a supermarket or anywhere where you meet people, because your immunity is nil. Having accepted these conditions I suddenly thought of something that I *could* do. I could write a book!

From the start I insisted that they put the drip in my left arm on treatment days which gave me free use of my right arm for writing, and in between hospital visits, while I was confined to the house, I could type it up on a lap-top.

One of the worst side effects of chemotherapy is that the body naturally rejects these strange chemicals being inserted into the bloodstream, so that at the height of the treatment you have to visit the bathroom every ten minutes all through the night. At this time I pushed all current thoughts from my mind and concentrated on reviving past memories. As soon as one of these manifested itself I would write it in a notebook which I kept by the bed. This worked well so that I was able to recall such otherwise forgotten details as names and places.

The best progress I was able to make was during the four days of taking steroids. These are prescribed to help you through the worst time that follows each treatment. The sensation is most unreal. You feel as though you are floating about ten feet in the air, but you are still able to concentrate on the task of typing.

I have never taken drugs in my life, and if this is anything like the effect of drug taking, then I never will. I cannot understand how anyone would want to voluntarily subject themselves to such a false sense of euphoria. For me the reality of tackling life's ups and downs and eventually succeeding is much more rewarding than temporarily insulating yourself from them.

I made an attempt about twenty years ago to write my autobiography, but just at the point when the manuscript was 'print-ready' the publisher went bankrupt, and it was abandoned. During the enforced confinement of treatment and subsequent convalescence, the book of my childhood gradually manifested itself. The situation gave me the opportunity to describe my early life and thus provide a natural introduction to the possible rebirth of the autobiography.

So that is how this book came to be written. I do not recommend contracting cancer, but if you are one of the three, who does, then try writing a book. The process takes your mind off the unpleasant experience and gives you a positive goal to aim for!

This book has been my story from birth, through school, through teenage, into wage earning, and on to the world of commerce. What has surprised me the most is how an old man, who regularly loses his car keys, is still able to remember such details, especially people's names! Forgive me if I just say "Hallo!" when we meet tomorrow, because I probably will not remember yours!

The other thing that is surprising is that the longest chapter is chapter one, 'Pre-school', considering that I went to an infants' school at the age of four! I do not know at what age a baby becomes aware of its surroundings, but you would certainly not think that those few years would have left such an impression!

Looking again at the drawings which I did as a teenager, and that are reproduced in this book, I realize that I drew no more after the age of seventeen. I think that I have to blame motorcycles again for this curtailment of my artistic leanings. If I had not put my pencil down and had held a motorcycle twist grip instead, then who knows what direction my career would have taken? Maybe some pictures in the National Gallery instead of entries in The Guinness Book of Records!

This film impressed me, probably because he was so much better looking than me!

The MotoCyclons at the peak of their popularity in the late 60's.

Moving on, the book finishes up during my time at Whitepost Garage. Working hard repairing cars in the winter and presenting motorcycle stunt shows in the summer, when a life-changing incident occurred! I had not been paid for my performance at a small village show and this rankled with me. My agent, Mr. Bert Layton, tried to persuade me to join the Variety Artists Federation, but I was not particularly interested. I had to be in a union during my time at G.A.C., and they did not seem to do much for me, but when he said that one of the things that they could do was to fight for unpaid performing fees, I immediately took an interest!

I joined and they got me my money, and then the biggest bonus of all, was that they were absorbed by The British Actors Equity Association. This is a union which is renowned for being very difficult to join, but I was handed a full Equity card straight away and I am still a lifetime member to this day! I can walk onto a film set in Gloucester docks and I could have a walk-on part in preference to all the other people hoping to get on TV who do not have an Equity card. The pay is about £10 an hour, plus food, which is minimal in comparison to the thousands that my membership has brought me over the years! Another example of the truth behind that old adage is, 'Being in the right place at the right time!'

To read all about those years and the astounding behind the scenes stories, you must read my autobiography. It is called 'Close to the Edge' and is unique in many ways. It is in fact a duo-autobiography, because it is by Jacquie De Creed and me. Just one special aspect is that we both hold world records that almost certainly will never be beaten! Mine is that of walking away from 2003 auto wrecks in a stunting career. The next nearest is hundreds behind and will never catch up. Hers is that of driving a car off a ramp at 130 m p h and achieving an incredible leap of 232 feet and one inch at Santa Pod Raceway in 1983, and driving on after landing! For those of you who only understand metres it is the length of seven London buses end to end. No man or woman has ever leaped a car or motorcycle further, in spite of several attempts worldwide!

There was a T. V. programme called The Guinness Book of Records that claimed that an Australian had broken it, but it was just hype. We managed to obtain a tape of the attempt and had it professionally analysed. Knowing the model of car he used, they were able to calculate all the measurements. Real-time photography gives you all the other information you need. From these calculations they were able to tell us that his maximum speed was 90 m p h, and that the distance from the tip of the ramp to the point of landing was no more than 90 feet!

We also learned that he injured himself on landing, and that it occurred on a practice run the day before his official attempt. There were no spectators present, only his team and the film crew. We think that the program makers were so sorry for him, because he had made several attempts in the past and failed, that they decided to be kind, and say that he had achieved it. This false record was rescinded before the next edition and Jacquie was restored supreme!

If you want to attempt to break a world record then any edition of The Guinness Book of Records will explain how in the first few pages. The most important thing is to tell them of your attempt in advance to give them the opportunity of attending. You must also have it fully adjudicated by a responsible body, with as much film and photo back-up as possible. The authenticity of the book relies on it being fair and true!

Norris McWhirter, the original joint editor with his brother Ross, was kind enough to write a glowing foreword for 'Close to the Edge'. There are many other famous characters featured. The indomitable Murray Walker, the motor race commentator, actually did the commentary for one of our record attempts, and Sir Terry Wogan did a voice-over for one of our commercials.

So, if you have enjoyed this book, and want to learn how my career in show business progressed, then your next book has to be 'Close to the Edge'!

'HUNTING THE MOOSE

My canoe and my Boy Scout knife probably inspired my
teenage imagination to create this exotic drawing.